ROOTS OF WISDOM: UNDERSTANDING INDIAN KNOWLEDGE SYSTEM

DR. ALOK TRIPATHI
PALLAVI TRIPATHI

This Book is dedicated to my Family & Students

Contents

Preface

The Indian Knowledge System (IKS) stands as a monumental and interdisciplinary tradition, bringing together profound insights across philosophy, science, mathematics, art, governance, medicine, and spirituality. Developed over millennia, it is a legacy that has inspired not only the Indian subcontinent but also civilizations around the world. Through an extensive collection of texts, oral traditions, and philosophical discussions, IKS has contributed in essential ways to global intellectual heritage. This book seeks to provide a comprehensive journey through these rich traditions, elucidating the historical roots, cultural significance, and enduring relevance of Indian Knowledge Systems.

In exploring the broad landscape of IKS, the book opens with an overview of its early origins, touching upon the Vedic literature, the Upanishads, and the major schools of Indian philosophy. The Vedas, dating back over three millennia, mark one of humanity's earliest literary accomplishments, containing reflections on cosmology, ethics, and metaphysics. Complementing these are the Upanishads, whose focus on the nature of consciousness and self-realization have left an indelible mark on philosophical traditions worldwide. Through such texts, Indian thinkers have posed questions on the nature of existence, knowledge, and morality—questions that continue to echo through philosophical inquiry today.

Following the philosophical framework, the book delves into the Dharma Shastra, the ancient Indian treatises on law and ethics. These texts, such as the Manusmriti, delineate a comprehensive social and legal code that governed personal, familial, and societal conduct, with a focus on the concept of dharma, or righteous duty. Such guidelines laid the foundation for ethical and legal systems that resonated across centuries and continue to influence modern discussions on ethics and justice. Similarly, the Artha Shastra, attributed to the sage and advisor Kautilya, presents a sophisticated approach to governance and economics, offering invaluable insights into statecraft, diplomacy, and the art of resource management that remain pertinent in today's global political and economic contexts.

The journey through IKS would be incomplete without attention to its artistic and aesthetic dimensions, which are represented through the Natya Shastra. As the oldest surviving treatise on performing arts, it covers drama, music, and dance, establishing concepts like rasa, or emotional essence, that have shaped Indian and Southeast Asian art traditions for centuries. In architecture and spatial design, Vastu Shastra serves as an ancient guide, harmonizing human dwellings with cosmic principles to foster balance, health, and prosperity. Its influence endures, as principles of Vastu are increasingly embraced in contemporary architecture and sustainable design practices.

The book also addresses the contributions of Jyotisha, the traditional Indian astronomical and astrological system that emphasized the interconnectedness of celestial movements and human affairs. The principles of Jyotisha, founded upon precise mathematical calculations, reveal ancient Indians' profound understanding of the cosmos. Likewise, Ayurveda, the holistic science of life, provides an approach to health that combines medical knowledge, lifestyle practices, and spirituality, aimed at achieving harmony between mind, body, and spirit. The revival of

Ayurveda in modern healthcare systems worldwide underscores its relevance in addressing today's health challenges.

In addition to discussing each of these fields in detail, this book highlights the interdisciplinary approach inherent in IKS. Indian knowledge traditions rarely confined themselves to isolated disciplines; instead, they integrated insights across fields, fostering a holistic understanding that is increasingly relevant in a world where multifaceted approaches are vital to solving complex issues. The Indian Knowledge System's emphasis on balance, sustainability, and ethical responsibility aligns with current movements toward environmental awareness, mental health, and social justice.

This book is an invitation to rediscover an invaluable intellectual legacy. It aims to provide not only an understanding of Indian Knowledge Systems but also a sense of their contemporary applications. As modern education moves toward inclusive, interdisciplinary learning, this exploration of IKS will resonate with students, scholars, and anyone seeking a deeper appreciation of India's cultural and intellectual contributions to humanity. It is my hope that this text will inspire further study, bridging the ancient and the modern in ways that bring meaningful insights to the challenges and possibilities of the present and future.

Acknowledgements

This book would not have been possible without the support, guidance, and encouragement of numerous individuals and institutions who contributed in invaluable ways to its conception, research, and completion. My heartfelt gratitude goes to each person and organization that has shared their time, expertise, and belief in the importance of this project.

Firstly, I extend my deepest appreciation to my mentors and academic colleagues who offered their insight, advice, and constructive feedback throughout the research and writing process. Their extensive knowledge of the Indian Knowledge System (IKS), paired with their dedication to preserving and sharing this rich cultural heritage, has greatly inspired me. I am particularly grateful to those who generously shared their perspectives and ideas, broadening my understanding and appreciation for the intricacies of IKS. Their ongoing encouragement and guidance have been instrumental, reminding me of the significance of this work in highlighting a knowledge tradition that continues to shape and influence global thought.

My sincerest thanks are also owed to the scholars and researchers whose pioneering work laid the foundation for this book. Their commitment to exploring, preserving, and revitalizing Indian Knowledge Systems has been invaluable, providing both a roadmap and a wealth of information that enabled me to approach this subject with respect and depth. Their contributions are an evidence to the enduring relevance of these knowledge systems, and their learning has been both inspiring and foundational in bringing this work to completion.

I am profoundly grateful to my family and friends, whose unwavering support and understanding have sustained me throughout this journey. Their patience during the long hours of research and writing, along with their encouragement during moments of challenge, have been crucial. I am especially thankful for their faith in the value and impact of this work. To my family, who instilled in me a love for learning and a respect for the wisdom of our heritage, thank you for fostering an environment that celebrates intellectual curiosity and cultural appreciation. I am equally thankful to my friends, who were always there to motivate me and remind me of the importance of this project.

This book has also greatly benefited from the resources provided by libraries, archives, and institutions. My thanks go to the dedicated librarians and archivists who assisted me in locating rare and essential texts, allowing me access to invaluable primary sources and research materials. Their efforts to preserve and organize vast bodies of knowledge are commendable, and without these resources, this book would lack the depth and historical context that these institutions have made available. Special appreciation is owed to the institutions that maintain collections of ancient manuscripts and texts, as their work has ensured that these materials are accessible to future generations of scholars.

I would also like to acknowledge the invaluable contributions of the editorial team and the publishing house, whose expertise and dedication have significantly enhanced the quality of this book. Their meticulous attention to detail, thoughtful suggestions, and commitment to excellence have elevated this project, ensuring that it resonates with readers while preserving the academic rigor that the subject demands. I am grateful for their support in bringing this book to its final form, and for their belief in its relevance and potential impact.

Finally, I must acknowledge the ancient scholars, thinkers, and visionaries who contributed to the Indian Knowledge System centuries ago. Their works have left an enduring legacy, inspiring generations and offering timeless wisdom that continues to be of immense value. Through their dedication to learning, inquiry, and ethical principles, these ancient luminaries have paved the way for modern scholarship and understanding, providing us with insights into human experience, the natural world, and the pursuit of truth. It is their work that made this exploration of IKS possible, and I am deeply grateful to be part of the continuing journey to honor and share their insights with the world.

To everyone who has supported, encouraged, and guided me in this endeavor, I extend my deepest and most sincere gratitude. This book is a tribute to each of you and to the collective efforts that have made it possible.

CHAPTER ONE

Overview and Significance of the Indian Knowledge System

Introduction

Indian Knowledge System (IKS) is a rich and diverse pool of knowledge that has developed over a long period of time covering multiple subjects like philosophy, science, arts, administration, health, mathematics, religion and so on. It is much older than six centuries and has contributed and still contributes to the knowledge systems of the world. Numerous Indian Knowledge Systems have been codified and transmitted in the forms of texts, oral traditions and discussions. They elaborate on the state of man, reality and the place of an individual in the universe. This chapter examines the overall landscape of the Indian Knowledge System, its growth, major achievements and importance in modern times.

Historical Evolution of the Indian Knowledge System

The composition of the Vedas, the founding books of the Indian Knowledge System, occurred during the Vedic era, which began approximately 1500 BCE. These scriptures, especially the Rig Veda, have songs that describe creation, the divine, and human life. They also contain hymns that encapsulate cosmic knowledge. An early awareness of many scientific ideas is seen in the Vedas' allusions to astronomy, medicine, agriculture, mathematics, and science. From 800 to 400 BCE, the Upanishads were composed, expanding upon the philosophical and metaphysical concepts introduced in the Vedas. They explored in further detail the concepts of the soul (Atman), the nature of reality (Brahman), and the cycle of life and death (Samsara). Many people believe that the Upanishadic era marked the start of a more structured system of Indian philosophy.

The emergence of several philosophical systems, including Nyaya, Vaisheshika, Sankhya, Yoga, Mimamsa, and Vedanta, contributed to the expansion of Indian Knowledge Systems. Fundamental issues in logic, ethics, epistemology, and metaphysics were discussed in these schools. In a similar vein, the introduction of Buddhism and Jainism in the sixth century BCE gave Indian intellectual discourse new perspectives. The Gupta period (320-550 CE) is often regarded as the "Golden Age" of Indian science, notably in mathematics, astronomy, and medicine. During this time, scholars like as Aryabhata and Varahamihira contributed much to astronomy and mathematics. Similarly, the ancient work "Sushruta Samhita" became a seminal treatise on medicine and surgery.

Components of the Indian Knowledge System

The Indian Knowledge System is interdisciplinary and may be divided into several components, each of which has helped to shape the intellectual and cultural framework of the Indian subcontinent.

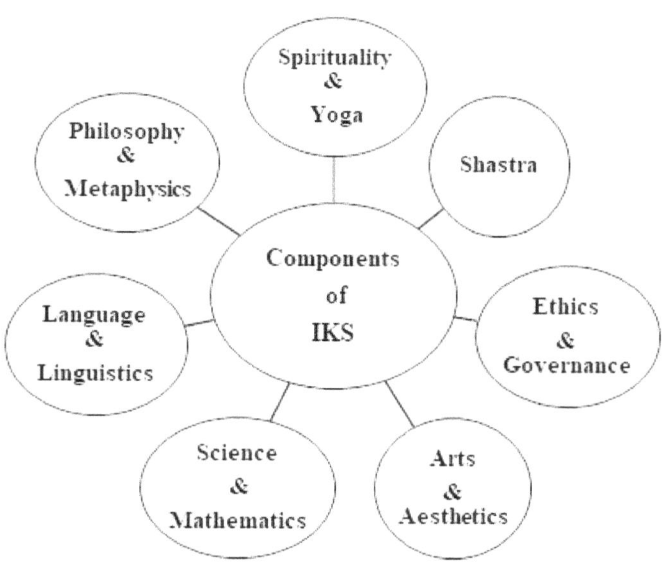

Various components of Indian Knwoledge System

Philosophy and Metaphysics

Indian philosophy involves many viewpoints on reality, knowledge, and ethics. The major schools of Indian philosophy—Nyaya, Vaisheshika, Samkhya, Yoga, Purva Mimamsa, and Vedanta—along with Buddhist and Jain traditions, provided a rich intellectual environment for debates about the nature of life, awareness, and the self. Vedanta, for example, stressed non-dualism (Advaita), implying that the individual soul (Atman) and the global soul (Brahman) are same. In contrast, the Nyaya School emphasized logical reasoning and epistemology, attempting to establish truth by rational inquiry.

Science and Mathematics

India's contributions to arithmetic, astronomy, and science have had a significant influence on the world's intellectual history. The notion of zero, the decimal system, algebraic equations, and the Pythagorean Theorem all have their origins in ancient Indian mathematics. Aryabhata, Brahmagupta, and Bhaskara II were innovators in these domains. Astronomically, the prehistoric era Indians had a thorough grasp of planetary movements, the solar year, and lunar cycles. Aryabhata's research on the rotation of the Earth and the calculation of the value of pi was remarkable. In addition to astronomy and mathematics, Ayurveda, India's ancient medical system, has been practiced for millennia. It combines biology, pharmacology, and physiology concepts while emphasizing the importance of body element balance (Vata, Pitta, and Kapha) in health and wellbeing.

Language and Linguistics

Sanskrit, India's classical language, played an important role in knowledge retention and transfer. It is sometimes referred to as a "perfect" language due to its systematic grammar, which was documented by the ancient grammarian Panini in his fundamental work, Ashtadhyayi. Panini's understanding of grammar, linguistic systems, and syntax is still unequaled and has influenced current linguistics. Sanskrit books include a vast range of topics, from philosophy to law, poetry, and science. In besides Sanskrit, Prakrit and Pali were important languages that influenced Buddhist and Jain literature.

Arts and Aesthetics

Indian Knowledge Systems include significant aesthetic and artistic philosophies. Bharata's Natya Shastra is a basic work for dramaturgy, dance, and performance arts. It developed the notion of "rasa" (aesthetic essence), which divides emotions into nine categories and influenced both art and literature. These aesthetic elements underpin Indian classical music, dance, sculpture, and painting.

Ethics and Governance

The Indian Knowledge System provides extensive viewpoints on government, ethics, and the law. Kautilya (also known as Chanakya) wrote the Arthashastra in the fourth century BCE as a book on statecraft, economics, and military tactics. It defines leadership, political diplomacy, and warfare, emphasizing the need of governance in sustaining societal order.Similarly, the Dharmashastra writings examine ethics, morality, and legal systems, offering guidance for personal and community behavior. They stress Dharma (goodness) as the cornerstone for a fair society.

Spirituality and Yoga

Yoga, one of the most widely recognized components of the Indian Knowledge System, involves more than just physical postures; it also encompasses a full philosophy of self-discipline, ethical behavior, and spiritual freedom. Patanjali's Yoga Sutras establish the eight-fold path (Ashtanga Yoga), which includes moral standards (Yama and Niyama), physical postures (Asanas), breath control (Pranayama), and meditation (Dhyana). India's spiritual knowledge encompasses a variety of worship styles, ceremonial activities, and pathways to enlightenment. The Bhagavad Gita, for example, explains the essence of responsibility, devotion, and the path of knowledge, directing people to self-realization.

Shastra

"**Shastra**" (Sanskrit: शास्त्र) is a Sanskrit term that refers to a set of rules, instructions, teachings, or treatises on a particular field of knowledge. It is often translated as "scripture" or "treatise" in English, but its meaning goes beyond religious texts, encompassing a wide range of disciplines including science, art, law, philosophy, and governance. Key Meanings of Shastra:

i. **Scripture or Sacred Text**: In religious and spiritual contexts, Shastra often refers to the sacred texts of Hinduism, Buddhism, and Jainism, which provide guidance on how to live according to religious principles. Examples include the **Dharma Shastra**, which deals with ethics and laws, and **Yoga Shastra**, which addresses practices of yoga.

ii. **Record on a Subject**: In a more general sense, Shastra refers to a comprehensive and authoritative text on any subject. It can cover fields like:

- **Artha Shastra**: A treatise on governance, politics, and economics, traditionally attributed to Kautilya (Chanakya).
- **Natya Shastra**: A text on performing arts, including dance, drama, and music, attributed to the sage Bharata.
- **Vastu Shastra**: A traditional Indian system of architecture and spatial design.
- **Jyotisha Shastra**: A text on astrology and astronomy.
- **Ayurveda Shastra**: A treatise on traditional Indian medicine and healthcare.

i. **Body of Knowledge or Discipline**: Shastra can also denote a structured system of knowledge or science. For instance, the term **Vidya Shastra** refers to the science of knowledge, and **Rasa Shastra** refers to the knowledge of alchemy and chemistry in the traditional Indian context.

ii. **Law or Rule**: In ancient Indian traditions, Shastras often played the role of legal and moral codes, guiding human behavior in both personal and societal contexts. For example, the **Manusmriti** or **Manava Dharma Shastra** is a text that outlines the laws governing human conduct, social order, and justice.

Characteristics of a Shastra:

- **Systematic and Authoritative**: A Shastra provides a detailed, organized framework for understanding and practicing a particular domain of knowledge. It is considered authoritative and is often based on traditional wisdom accumulated over centuries.

- **Based on Principles**: Shastras are not random collections of ideas but are rooted in principles or laws that govern a particular field, whether it's science, art, or spirituality.
- **Transmitted Through Generations**: Many Shastras have been preserved and passed down through oral traditions, manuscripts, and teachings over thousands of years in Indian civilization.

Examples of Shastras:

- **Dharma Shastra**: Texts dealing with law, ethics, and moral duties. Examples include the *Manusmriti* and *Yajnavalkya Smriti*.
- **Artha Shastra**: A treatise on politics, economics, and military strategy, attributed to the ancient Indian philosopher Kautilya.
- **Shilpa Shastra**: Texts dealing with arts, crafts, and architecture, especially temple construction.
- **Nyaya Shastra**: Texts on logic and reasoning, part of the Indian philosophical tradition.

The Role of Oral Traditions in the Indian Knowledge System

One of the distinctive features of the Indian information System is its dependence on oral traditions for information transfer. Long before written books appeared, the insight of the Vedas and other early scriptures was passed down from generation to generation by oral recital and memory. This method of transmission not only preserved great volumes of information, but also secured its survival across millennia. The Gurukul educational system was crucial to this oral transmission, with pupils (shishyas) living with their teachers (gurus) and learning via direct teaching and repetition. Texts such as the Vedas were spoken with exact phonetic articulation and rhythm to ensure that information was transferred correctly. This approach encouraged strong relationships between teachers and students, resulting in a comprehensive environment for intellectual and spiritual development. Oral transmission also allowed for some degree of freedom and interpretation. While the Vedas' essential principles were retained, succeeding academics such as Adi Shankaracharya, Ramanujacharya, and others expanded on the legacy by adapting it to contemporary situations and philosophical discussions.

Ancient Gurukul Education System

Preservation of knowledge through manuscripts

In conjunction with oral traditions, the creation of written writings in India greatly increased the breadth and retention of knowledge. Palm leaf manuscripts and birch bark were popular writing materials, and scribes carefully copied texts to preserve continuity. Major institutions such as Nalanda, Takshashila, and Vikramashila were hubs for the compilation and study of these works. They drew intellectuals from across Asia, helping to the diffusion of Indian knowledge outside the subcontinent. The safeguarding of Indian knowledge through manuscripts was a massive undertaking, since so much of the early literature was prone to degradation owing to the fragility of the materials utilized. This has caused issues for current academics attempting to rebuild old knowledge systems. Many of these texts have been lost throughout centuries due to invasions, weather, and neglect. However, initiatives by Indian institutions and governments have resulted in the digitalization of manuscripts, assuring their preservation for years to come.

Contributions to Education and Pedagogy

The Indian Knowledge System made a significant contribution towards the creation of educational techniques. The Gurukul method stressed experiential learning, which focused not on rote memorizing but on grasping the underlying concepts of topics. In addition to intellectual activities, students were taught critical thinking, ethics, and self-discipline. Besides intellectual and spiritual teachings, the curriculum included practical skills like as metallurgy, agriculture, navigation, and the arts. This comprehensive education produced individuals with diverse backgrounds who could positively impact society in a variety of ways. The focus on Sadhana (personal practice and discipline) was critical in this philosophy, since knowledge was viewed not only as academic achievement but also as a way of self-transformation. The Indian Knowledge System also promoted the idea of lifelong learning. The Upanishads, for example, emphasize the ongoing quest of knowledge and wisdom, depicting life as a never-ending learning process. This approach is consistent with current educational principles that promote lifelong learning as a means of adapting to a constantly changing reality.

Interdisciplinary Approach in the Indian Knowledge System

One of the advantages of the Indian Knowledge System is its intrinsic multidisciplinary character. There was no clear distinction between different domains of study. As an illustration, the study of philosophy was frequently linked with metaphysics, ethics, logic, and religion, reflecting a comprehensive understanding of human existence. Similarly, medicine (Ayurveda) was associated with spirituality, emphasizing the relationship between body, mind, and soul. This cross-disciplinary strategy enabled the emergence of numerous intellectual traditions, with different disciplines of knowledge viewed as interrelated rather than isolated realms. The Charaka Samhita and Sushruta Samhita, basic works in medicine, drew from philosophy, metaphysics, and biology, whilst Vastu Shastra (architecture) combined aesthetics, cosmology, and mathematics. The ancient notion of Jyotisha, or Indian astrology, which merged astronomy with spiritual activities, is another example of a fusion of disciplines. This comprehensive vision, which does not compartmentalize information, is still applicable today, since current fields understand the need of interdisciplinary study.

Ecology and Sustainability in Indian Knowledge Systems

Even prior to current environmental movements began, the Indian Knowledge System understood the need of sustainability and ecological balance. The Vedas and other ancient literature frequently discuss the interconnection of all living things, emphasizing the significance of living in balance with nature. The cosmic order, suggests that the cosmos obeys natural principles, and that humanity must follow these laws in order to exist healthily. The discipline of Ahimsa (nonviolence), which is promoted by both Jainism and Buddhism, applies to all living beings and demonstrates a deep regard for life. This ethical concept also influences ecological practices since it encourages the reduction of harm to animals and the environment. An in-depth knowledge of natural cycles served as the foundation for many ancient Indian agricultural techniques, including crop rotation and organic farming. The Science of Plants, or Vrikshayurveda, is an ancient literature that describes techniques for managing water, conserving soil, and practicing sustainable agriculture. In the modern world, when addressing environmental degradation and climate change is becoming increasingly important, these sustainability concepts are finding newfound significance.

Medicine and Well-Being: Ayurveda

The foundation of the Indian Knowledge System is Ayurveda, one of the world's oldest medical systems. Its foundations are found in the Atharva Veda, and it was methodically developed in writings like the Sushruta Samhita and Charaka Samhita. In addition to being a medical system, Ayurveda is a way of life that emphasizes preserving harmony between the body, mind, and spirit for overall wellbeing. The preventative as well as the therapeutic nature of Ayurvedic medicine stems from its emphasis on the balance of the three doshas (Vata, or air, Pitta, or fire), and Kapha, or water and earth), as well as the idea of Prakriti, or one's inherent constitution. The particular arrangement of these components defines the physical and mental well-being of each person. Ayurveda places a strong emphasis on individualized care, nutrition control, and lifestyle modifications. It frequently uses yoga and meditation as healing modalities.

Ayurveda is still relevant for treating contemporary health issues, as evidenced by the worldwide upsurge of interest in it. Ayurvedic medicine provides a more holistic approach to health, concentrating on the underlying causes of disease and fostering wellbeing rather than just treating symptoms, in response to growing concerns about the shortcomings of allopathic medicine, particularly in managing chronic diseases and mental health difficulties.

Indian Knowledge Systems' Influence on World Thinking

Indian knowledge, especially through trade routes and cultural exchanges, has had a significant impact on other civilizations. For instance, Indian astronomy and mathematics were brought to the Islamic world, where academics translated Indian writings into Arabic, impacting the advancement of science throughout the Islamic Golden Age of the Middle Ages. Mathematical history was changed when ideas like zero and the decimal system were introduced to Europe and went on to alter mathematics. East Asian civilizations were greatly influenced by Indian philosophy, especially Buddhism, which had a profound effect on the spiritual and cultural advancement of China, Japan, Korea, and Southeast Asia. Similar to this, the merging of Indian and Central Asian cultural forms was made easier by the Silk Road's dissemination of Indian literature, art, and architecture.

Indian spiritual concepts were a source of inspiration for Western philosophers and authors in the 19th and 20th centuries. Indian philosophy was cited by authors such as Ralph Waldo Emerson, Henry David Thoreau, and Carl Jung. Swami Vivekananda's exposition of the non-dualist Advaita Vedanta teachings had a particularly profound effect on the Western conception of spirituality.

Reviving and Integrating Indian Knowledge Systems in Modern Education

In contemporary India, there is growing recognition of the need to integrate the Indian Knowledge System into modern educational frameworks. For a long time, the colonial education system imposed Western paradigms, often neglecting India's indigenous intellectual heritage. However, recent initiatives are aimed at incorporating aspects of Indian philosophy, linguistics, arts, and sciences into the curriculum. Organizations and scholars are working to preserve and promote Sanskrit and other classical languages, which are critical for accessing ancient texts. Efforts are also underway to digitize manuscripts and create research programs dedicated to exploring the contributions of Indian knowledge to global intellectual history. Moreover, Indian universities are beginning to offer interdisciplinary programs that combine traditional knowledge with modern research methods. This allows students to explore fields like Ayurveda, Yoga, and Vedic mathematics alongside contemporary scientific and social theories.

Contemporary Relevance of the Indian Knowledge System

The Indian Knowledge System is very important in the current world for solving contemporary problems. Ayurveda's emphasis on preventative healthcare and holistic approach provide insightful information for enhancing world health. Yoga, on the other hand, has become a worldwide craze for encouraging a balanced lifestyle due to its emphasis on both mental and physical well-being. Ancient Indian philosophical contentions on human responsibility, awareness, and the nature of reality have influenced modern conversations about artificial intelligence, consciousness, and environmental ethics. Because of its exact language structure, Sanskrit studies has also had an impact on disciplines like artificial intelligence and computational linguistics. The development of Sanskrit-based algorithms for natural language processing (NLP) technologies highlights the value of Indian linguistic expertise in the contemporary digital era.

Challenges in Preserving the Indian Knowledge System

The Indian Knowledge System is large, yet it has many problems these days. Several indigenous knowledge traditions were interrupted by colonialism, and the concentration of the contemporary educational system on Western scientific paradigms frequently obscures the contributions of Indian intellectuals. Furthermore, a great deal of old manuscripts and books have been badly maintained or are not translated, which results in the loss of important knowledge. The Indian Knowledge System is being revived and incorporated into regular schooling. Important measures toward maintaining this intellectual legacy include the digitalization of manuscripts, multidisciplinary study, and the promotion of Sanskrit and other ancient languages.

Conclusion

The intellectual, spiritual, and scientific accomplishments of ancient and medieval India are attested to the Indian Knowledge System. It has made enormous contributions to knowledge across a wide range of disciplines, including philosophy, the arts, medicine, and mathematics. The ideas and understandings gained from this method are still applicable in today's society, providing answers to major issues and stimulating fresh perspectives. The Indian Knowledge System acts as a link between the ancient and the modern, the local and the global, as we progress toward a more integrated and comprehensive view of knowledge.

Shorts question

1. What are the four Vedas in the Indian Knowledge System, and what do they represent?
2. Which ancient Indian text is known for its contributions to economics and political science?
3. What is the central theme of the Upanishads in Indian philosophy?
4. How did Aryabhata contribute to the field of mathematics and astronomy in India?
5. What is the importance of Ayurveda in the Indian Knowledge System?
6. What does the term "Rasa" refer to in Indian aesthetics and performing arts?
7. Which text serves as the foundational guide for Vastu Shastra, the ancient Indian science of architecture?
8. What are the core concepts of Samkhya philosophy in the Indian Knowledge System?
9. How does the Indian Knowledge System integrate spiritual and scientific knowledge?

Descriptive questions

1. How has the Indian Knowledge System contributed to global scientific thought, particularly in fields such as mathematics and astronomy? Provide examples of key figures and texts that illustrate this influence?
2. In what ways does Ayurveda reflect the holistic approach of the Indian Knowledge System to health and wellness, and how does it differ from Western medical practices? Discuss its historical significance and modern applications.

3. Discuss the role of the Vedas and Upanishads in shaping the philosophical and spiritual landscape of India. How do these texts continue to influence contemporary thought and practices?

4. Examine the significance of the *Natya Shastra* in the context of Indian performing arts. How does this text contribute to the understanding of aesthetics, drama, and dance in Indian culture?

5. Analyze the principles of Vastu Shastra and their relevance in modern architecture and urban planning. How do these ancient guidelines promote harmony between built environments and nature?

6. What are the key contributions of Indian philosophers like Adi Shankaracharya and Ramanujacharya to the understanding of consciousness and the nature of reality? How do their ideas resonate with modern philosophical discourse?

7. Discuss the impact of Indian linguistics, particularly Panini's Ashtadhyayi, on the study of language and grammar worldwide. How has this ancient text influenced contemporary linguistic theory?

8. How do Indian traditional knowledge systems address environmental sustainability and agriculture? Explore specific practices or texts that emphasize ecological balance and sustainable living.

9. In what ways does the Indian Knowledge System integrate various disciplines such as philosophy, science, art, and spirituality? Provide examples of how this interdisciplinary approach enhances holistic understanding.

10. Reflect on the relevance of the Indian Knowledge System in the 21st century. How can its principles and insights inform contemporary challenges in education,

governance, and societal well-being?

CHAPTER TWO

Dharma Shastra: The Ancient Indian Legal and Ethical Tradition

The *Dharma Shastra* (Sanskrit: धर्मशास्त्र) is a body of literature in ancient Indian tradition that deals with law, ethics, and moral conduct. It forms the foundation of the legal and social order in ancient Indian society, encompassing a vast range of subjects, including duties, rights, justice, property, marriage, inheritance, and even penalties for crimes. These texts are part of the broader category of Hindu Shastras and are deeply rooted in Vedic principles. *Dharma* in the Indian context means duty, moral law, and righteousness. It is considered the guiding principle for living a life in harmony with the cosmic order, society, and one's personal roles. The *Shastra* (scripture) part indicates that these texts serve as formal treatises that provide comprehensive frameworks for the practice and understanding of *Dharma*.

This chapter explores the origin, scope, and significance of the *Dharma Shastra*, as well as the evolution of its principles and their influence on Indian society.

The Meaning and Scope of Dharma

The term "Dharma" has no single equivalent in Western languages, though it is often translated as "law," "duty," or "righteousness." It is a broader concept that refers to the moral principles governing the universe and human conduct. Dharma encompasses the following aspects:

- **Cosmic Law**: Dharma is the natural order of the universe that maintains balance and harmony. Everything in the cosmos, from celestial bodies to living creatures, operates within the framework of Dharma.
- **Social Duty**: Dharma refers to the responsibilities that individuals have toward society and their families. These duties are often linked to one's varna (class or caste) and ashrama (stage of life).
- **Personal Ethics**: On an individual level, Dharma involves living a life of virtue, practicing honesty, non-violence, compassion, and self-restraint.

The *Dharma Shastra* literature focuses on these aspects of Dharma and provides a detailed guide on how one should act in various situations to ensure the sustenance of the cosmic and social order.

Historical Evolution of Dharma Shastra

The *Dharma Shastra* texts are deeply connected to the Vedic tradition. While the earliest teachings on Dharma are found in the Vedas, particularly in the *Rigveda* and *Yajurveda*, the formal codification of these principles took place much later. The composition of the *Dharma Shastra* texts is traditionally attributed to sages who were considered to be wise lawgivers and scholars.

Origins in Vedic Literature

The concept of Dharma is rooted in Vedic thought. The Vedas, particularly the *Brahmanas* and *Aranyakas*, provide early references to the principles of moral and ethical conduct. However, the Dharma in these texts is primarily focused on ritualistic duties and obligations toward the gods.

Sutra Period (600–200 BCE)

The first systematic codifications of Dharma began during the Sutra period. The *Dharma Sutras*, which precede the *Dharma Shastra*, are concise manuals that form the foundation of the latter texts. These sutras were composed by different schools of thought and were generally brief in nature, often addressing legal and ethical matters related to rituals, conduct, and social norms. The most notable *Dharma Sutras* include:

- **Gautama Dharma Sutra**: One of the oldest known texts, addressing various aspects of duty, ritual, and law.
- **Apastamba Dharma Sutra**: Known for its emphasis on penance, ethics, and law.
- **Baudhāyana Dharma Sutra**: A text dealing with legal practices, rituals, and moral duties.
- **Vasistha Dharma Sutra**: Primarily focused on the duties of individuals and penalties for crimes.

Classical Period (200 BCE – 500 CE)

This period marks the flowering of *Dharma Shastra* literature, where the treatises became more elaborate and detailed. The most famous work from this era is the *Manu Smriti* or *Manava Dharma Shastra*, traditionally attributed to the sage Manu. This text played a significant role in shaping the legal and social frameworks of ancient India. Other important texts from this period include:

- **Yajnavalkya Smriti**: A text that rivals the *Manu Smriti* in authority and provides a more systematic approach to law and ethics.
- **Narada Smriti**: Focuses primarily on judicial procedures and the administration of justice.
- **Parashara Smriti**: Deals with Dharma applicable to the Kali Yuga, the current age of degeneration in Hindu cosmology.

Principles of Dharma Shastra

The *Dharma Shastra* texts cover a wide range of topics that can be grouped into four broad categories: personal conduct, social obligations, legal procedures, and penance.

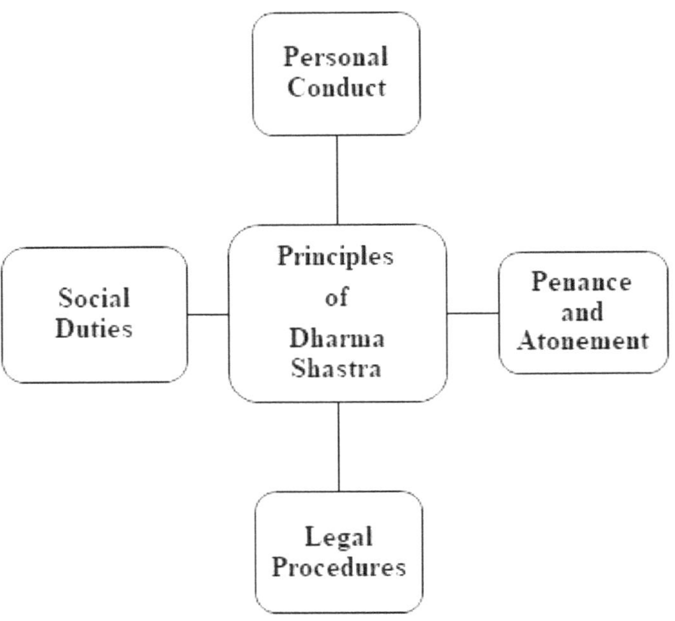

Principles of Dharma Shastra

Personal Conduct (Vyavahara)

Personal ethics are central to the teachings of the
Dharma Shastra. These texts provide guidelines for
righteous living, emphasizing virtues such as truthfulness
(*satya*), non-violence (*ahimsa*), self-discipline, and respect
for others. The texts also prescribe daily rituals, dietary
rules, and codes of behavior for individuals based on their
caste, gender, and stage of life.

Social Duties (Duties toward Family and Society)

The *Dharma Shastra* outlines the duties of individuals
based on their position in society, particularly in relation
to the caste system (varna) and the four stages of life

(ashrama). The four varnas are:

- **Brahmins**: Priests and scholars who are responsible for teaching and maintaining the spiritual and religious traditions.
- **Kshatriyas**: Warriors and rulers, responsible for governance, protection, and the enforcement of law.
- **Vaishyas**: Merchants and agriculturalists, responsible for trade and commerce.
- **Shudras**: Employers, artisans, and labourers.

The texts prescribe specific duties for each varna, with Brahmins being tasked with spiritual duties and teaching, while Kshatriyas are responsible for governance and protection. Vaishyas engage in trade and agriculture, while Shudras provide services to the other three classes.

In addition to varna, *Dharma Shastra* texts describe duties according to the four stages of life (ashramas):

- **Brahmacharya**: The stage of studentship and learning.
- **Grihastha**: The stage of household life, where one engages in family and social duties.
- **Vanaprastha**: The stage of retirement, where one renounces worldly attachments and focuses on spiritual pursuits.
- **Sannyasa**: The stage of renunciation, where one fully dedicates oneself to spiritual liberation.

Legal Procedures (Vyavahara)

The *Dharma Shastra* provides detailed guidelines on legal matters, including property rights, contracts, inheritance, and judicial procedures. These texts establish the framework for dealing with civil and criminal disputes and outline the qualifications of judges, the procedures for trials, and the appropriate punishments for various crimes. Judicial principles in the *Dharma Shastra* emphasize fairness, truthfulness, and the duty of the king or ruler to ensure justice. The texts advocate for the impartial administration of justice, with special attention given to protecting the rights of vulnerable members of society, such as women, children, and the elderly.

Penance and Atonement (Prayaschitta)

A unique aspect of the *Dharma Shastra* is its detailed treatment of penance and atonement. The texts outline specific practices for individuals who have committed moral or legal transgressions. These include various forms of atonement, such as fasting, giving charity, performing specific rituals, or, in extreme cases, voluntary exile or self-punishment.

Penance is seen as a means of purifying oneself and restoring harmony to both the individual and society. The severity of the penance prescribed depends on the nature of the offense and the status of the offender within the social hierarchy.

Manusmriti: The Most Influential Dharma Shastra

Among the *Dharma Shastra* texts, the *Manu Smriti*, or *Manava Dharma Shastra*, stands out as the most influential and widely cited text in the tradition. It is attributed to the sage Manu and is considered to be one of the earliest systematic codes of law and ethics in ancient India. The text is divided into twelve chapters and covers topics such as creation, the duties of different varnas, marriage, inheritance, governance, and the administration of justice. The *Manu Smriti* played a crucial role in shaping ancient and medieval Indian society. It was often cited by kings, legal scholars, and religious authorities to justify social norms and legal decisions.

However, it is also a controversial text, particularly in modern times, because of its strict prescriptions related to caste and gender roles. The text has been critiqued for reinforcing social inequalities and justifying discriminatory practices. Despite this, it remains a significant historical document for understanding the development of law and ethics in ancient India.

Contemporary Relevance of Dharma Shastra

While the *Dharma Shastra* texts were composed in a pre-modern context, their principles continue to influence contemporary Indian society, particularly in the fields of personal law and ethical conduct. Many aspects of Hindu personal law, especially those related to marriage, inheritance, and family life, are still informed by the principles outlined in these ancient texts.

Conclusion

A core component of Hindu philosophy, the Dharma Shastra provide a formalized framework for moral and legal behavior. They functioned as thorough guidelines for society order, justice, and government in addition to being morality manuals for individuals. Even though they are significant historically and culturally, they represent the patriarchal and hierarchical standards of ancient Indian culture, and their applicability in the modern period is frequently contested, particularly in light of caste and gender equality.

Short questions

1. What is Dharma Shastra, and what are its primary focuses?
2. Who is traditionally credited with the authorship of the Manusmriti, one of the most well-known Dharma Shastras?
3. How does Dharma Shastra define the concept of "Dharma" in relation to ethics and morality?
4. What the four main goals of life as outlined in the Dharma Shastras?
5. In what ways do Dharma Shastras address social hierarchies and caste systems in ancient India?
6. How does the *Manusmriti* discuss the roles and duties of men and women in society?
7. What is the significance of the concept of Karma in the context of Dharma Shastra?
8. How do Dharma Shastras approach the subject of law and justice in ancient Indian society?
9. What are some of the key differences between the various Dharma Shastras, such as the Manusmriti and the Yajnavalkya Smriti?
10. How have the interpretations of Dharma Shastra evolved in modern times, particularly in relation to contemporary legal and ethical issues?

Descriptive questions

1. Discuss the historical context in which the Dharma Shastras were written. How did the social, political, and cultural environments of ancient India shape their content and purpose?
2. Examine the concept of "Dharma" as presented in the Dharma Shastras. How do these texts define Dharma, and what factors influence its interpretation in different

contexts, such as personal ethics, social responsibilities, and legal obligations?

3. Analyze the role of the Manusmriti in shaping Indian legal traditions. How has this text influenced contemporary legal systems and ethical standards in India, and what are the criticisms of its interpretations?

4. Explore the significance of the four Purusharthas (goals of life) in the context of Dharma Shastra. How do these goals—Dharma, Artha, Kama, and Moksha—interrelate, and what guidance do the Dharma Shastras provide for achieving a balanced life?

5. Investigate the treatment of social hierarchy and caste in the Dharma Shastras. How do these texts justify the varna system, and what implications do they have for social organization and justice in ancient Indian society?

6. Discuss the gender roles outlined in the Dharma Shastras, particularly in texts like the Manusmriti. How do these texts address the duties and rights of women, and how have interpretations of these roles evolved over time?

7. Reflect on the relevance of Dharma Shastra in contemporary society. How can its principles inform modern discussions on ethics, law, and social justice, and what challenges arise in reconciling ancient texts with present-day values?

CHAPTER THREE

Artha Shastra: The Ancient Indian Science of Governance and Economics

The *Artha Shastra* (Sanskrit: अर्थशास्त्र) is an ancient Indian treatise on statecraft, economics, politics, military strategy, and law. Attributed to Kautilya (also known as Chanakya or Vishnugupta), a scholar, philosopher, and royal advisor during the reign of Emperor Chandragupta Maurya (circa 4th century BCE), this text is one of the oldest surviving works of political and economic thought in the world. The term "Artha" in Sanskrit means "wealth," "prosperity," or "meaning," while "Shastra" refers to "science" or "treatise." Thus, *Artha Shastra* can be translated as "the science of wealth" or "the science of material well-being." However, its scope extends far beyond economics, dealing with governance, diplomacy, espionage, legal systems, and military strategies to maintain a strong and prosperous state.

This chapter provides a comprehensive explanation of the *Artha Shastra*, including its historical context, key themes, and principles of governance, military strategies, and its relevance in contemporary political thought.

Historical Context of Artha Shastra

The *Artha Shastra* was written during a time of political fragmentation and instability in ancient India. Following the disintegration of the Nanda Empire, Chandragupta Maurya, with the guidance of his advisor Kautilya, rose to power and founded the Maurya Empire, one of the largest and most powerful empires in ancient India. Kautilya's *Artha Shastra* was crafted as a guide for rulers to help them navigate the complex political landscape and ensure the stability and prosperity of their kingdoms. The text remained lost for centuries, only to be rediscovered in 1905 by a scholar named R. Shamasastry, who translated it into English. Since then, the *Artha Shastra* has garnered significant interest from scholars of political science, economics, and international relations for its detailed and pragmatic approach to governance. While traditionally attributed to Kautilya, the text is likely a compilation of several layers of knowledge accumulated over centuries, reflecting the collective wisdom of Indian political thinkers.

The Structure and Content of Artha Shastra

The *Artha Shastra* is a voluminous text divided into 15 books (Adhikarnas), each dealing with different aspects of governance, administration, and military strategy. These books contain 180 chapters and cover a wide range of topics essential for ruling a state. The major areas covered in the text include:

1. **Kingship and Duties of the Ruler**: Guidance on how a ruler should govern justly and effectively.
2. **Administration**: Details on organizing bureaucracy, taxation, and the management of state finances.
3. **Diplomacy**: Strategies for forming alliances, conducting treaties, and negotiating with enemies.
4. **Espionage**: Methods for gathering intelligence and maintaining internal security.
5. **Law and Justice**: Legal procedures, punishment for crimes, and the role of the king as the ultimate judge.
6. **Military Strategy**: War tactics, defense, and expansion of the kingdom.

Each of these sections provides practical advice on how to maintain a prosperous and powerful state, with a particular emphasis on realpolitik, pragmatism, and the importance of maintaining law and order.

The Four Goals of Life

The *Artha Shastra* operates within the broader framework of the four traditional goals of life (*Purusharthas*) in Hindu philosophy: *Dharma* (duty, righteousness), *Artha* (wealth, prosperity), *Kama* (desire, pleasure), and *Moksha* (liberation, spiritual salvation). These goals represent the holistic balance that an individual must strive for in life. Kautilya focuses primarily on *Artha*, viewing wealth and power as essential means for ensuring social order and stability. However, he acknowledges the interconnection between all four goals, emphasizing that material prosperity (*Artha*) should be pursued within the boundaries of Dharma (ethical duty) to prevent societal chaos and maintain justice.

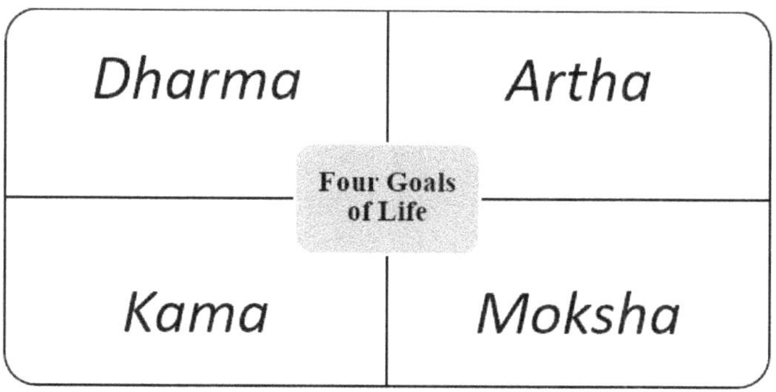

The four goals of life

Concepts in Arth Shastra

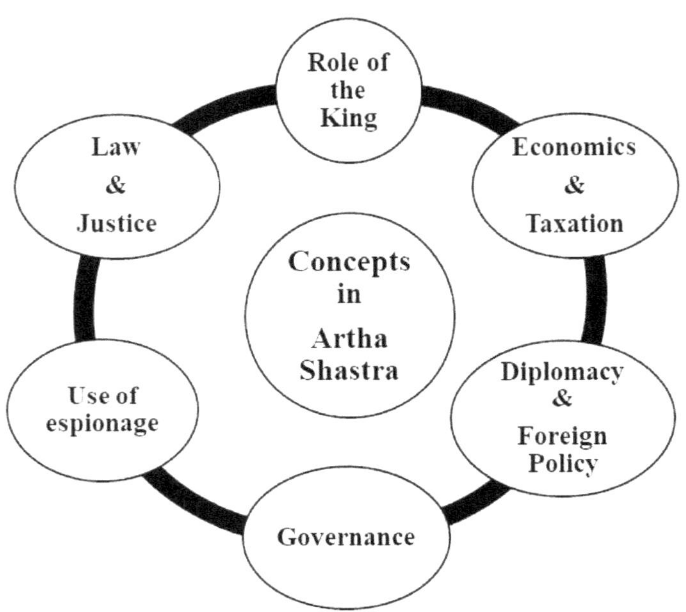

Central Concept of Artha Shastra

The Role of the King (Ruler)

At the heart of the *Artha Shastra* is the concept of kingship. Kautilya asserts that a king is central to the functioning of the state and is responsible for the welfare of his subjects. The text outlines the qualities a ruler must possess: intelligence, decisiveness, foresight, and a commitment to justice. The ruler must also balance power with ethical governance. While the accumulation of wealth and military strength is vital for maintaining the state, the king must not lose sight of his *Dharma* (moral obligations) to protect and serve his people. The king is advised to act with compassion and fairness, ensuring the well-being of all citizens, regardless of their social class.

Governance (Rajadharma)

Rajadharma, or the duty of a king, forms a crucial part of the *Artha Shastra*. Kautilya provides an elaborate guide for rulers on how to manage every aspect of the state, from appointing ministers to organizing bureaucratic departments. According to Kautilya, the state should be run with the help of a well-organized administrative system. The *Artha Shastra* advises that the kingdom should be divided into provinces, districts, and villages, each governed by officials who are accountable to higher authorities. The king is advised to regularly inspect the workings of his administration and ensure that corruption is kept in check.

Economics and Taxation

As its name suggests, *Artha Shastra* places significant emphasis on economics, trade, and wealth management. Kautilya believes that the prosperity of the state is linked directly to its wealth. He outlines methods for generating revenue, including efficient taxation systems, regulation of trade, and management of natural resources. One of the key principles in the text is that taxation should be fair and not overburden the population. The king is advised to extract taxes in such a way that the people continue to be productive and prosperous. A prosperous citizenry leads to a stronger, wealthier state, which in turn benefits the ruler.

Diplomacy and Foreign Policy

Kautilya's approach to foreign policy is pragmatic and sophisticated. He advocates a *mandala* theory of inter-state relations, which views politics as a web of alliances and enmities based on self-interest. According to this theory, neighboring states are potential enemies, while states further away may be considered allies. This system leads to a constant balancing of power through alliances, treaties, and military strategies. The *Artha Shastra* also advises rulers to use various diplomatic strategies based on context, including negotiation (*sandhi*), military force (*vigraha*), and fostering division within enemy ranks (*bheda*). Kautilya encourages the use of intelligence and espionage as essential tools in diplomacy to gain the upper hand.

The use of espionage

Espionage plays a crucial role in Kautilya's political philosophy. He advocates for a well-organized and covert network of spies who can provide the king with crucial information about enemies, internal dissent, and even the conduct of ministers and officials. Spies are employed not only to gather intelligence but also to spread disinformation and create divisions among rivals. Kautilya considers espionage a key element in maintaining control over both external threats and internal dissent. The system of spies is seen as a way to prevent corruption within the administration and to keep the ruler informed about the sentiments of the population.

Law and Justice

The *Artha Shastra* provides detailed guidance on the legal system of the state. It emphasizes that the king, as the ultimate authority, must ensure justice for all citizens. Kautilya outlines procedures for settling disputes, property rights, marriage laws, and criminal justice. Punishments for crimes are prescribed according to the severity of the offense, and the law is expected to be applied uniformly across all classes of society. The text advocates for harsh punishments as a deterrent for criminal behavior but also emphasizes fairness and due process. Judges and officials responsible for administering justice are expected to be impartial and free from corruption.

Military Strategy and Warfare

The *Artha Shastra* contains extensive discussions on military strategy, reflecting Kautilya's belief that a strong military is essential for the survival and expansion of the state. The text provides detailed instructions on the organization of armies, fortifications, war strategies, and the use of various weapons.

War Ethics and Strategy

Kautilya outlines the conditions under which war is justified and the strategies that should be employed. While he advocates for peaceful solutions through diplomacy whenever possible, he also emphasizes the importance of being prepared for war. Kautilya is realistic and pragmatic in his approach to warfare, advising rulers to use deception, psychological tactics, and even unconventional warfare to gain the upper hand.

The Role of the Military

The military is viewed as a vital part of the state, and the text discusses how the army should be structured and trained. Kautilya stresses the importance of discipline within the military ranks and the need for capable leadership. The army should be prepared for both defensive and offensive operations, with a clear understanding of the enemy's strengths and weaknesses.

Artha Shastra and Machiavelli: A Comparative Study

Kautilya's *Artha Shastra* is often compared to Niccolò Machiavelli's *The Prince*, a 16th-century European treatise on political strategy. Both works emphasize the importance of pragmatism in governance and suggest that rulers must sometimes use cunning, deceit, and force to maintain power. However, while Machiavelli's work is more focused on individual leadership, Kautilya's *Artha Shastra* presents a more comprehensive blueprint for the governance of the state as a whole, incorporating economic, legal, and social policies.

The comparison of Kautilya's Artha Shastra (written in ancient India, around 3rd century BCE) and Niccolò Machiavelli's The Prince (written in Renaissance Italy, 16th century CE) reveals striking similarities and differences in their approaches to political theory and statecraft, despite being written in vastly different cultural and temporal contexts. Both texts are considered pragmatic guides for rulers, focusing on power, governance, and realpolitik, but their worldviews and prescriptions differ in key ways.

<u>Similarities</u>

- **Realpolitik and Pragmatism:** Both Artha Shastra and The Prince focus on a pragmatic, sometimes ruthless, approach to governance. They recognize that rulers must sometimes act immorally or deceptively to maintain power and protect the state. Artha Shastra suggests that a king should act in his own interest, even if it involves duplicity, espionage, and using force. Similarly, Machiavelli is often associated with the principle that "the ends justify the means," recommending that rulers should not shy away from cruelty or deceit if it ensures stability and power.

- Focus on Power and Stability: Both texts prioritize the consolidation of power and the stability of the state as paramount. They see political power as the central goal of rulership. For Kautilya, ensuring the prosperity of the state is key, and he discusses the importance of military strength, economic management, and alliances. Machiavelli focuses on the acquisition, exercise, and preservation of political power, often through manipulation, strategy, and calculated decisions.

- **Statecraft and Military Power:** Both authors emphasize the importance of military strength in sustaining rule. The Artha Shastra devotes significant attention to strategies of warfare, alliances, and military management, detailing tactics for both offensive and defensive warfare.Similarly, Machiavelli advocates for rulers to maintain strong armies and to be prepared for war, even in times of peace.
- **Use of Deception and Espionage:** Kautilya places great emphasis on the use of spies, deceit, and intelligence-gathering as essential tools for a ruler.Machiavelli also advises rulers to be cunning and to manipulate perceptions, arguing that appearances can often be more important than reality when securing power.

<u>Differences</u>

- **Moral Framework:** Kautilya's Artha Shastra is grounded in the dharma (moral and social duties) of a ruler, even though it recognizes that rulers sometimes need to act immorally for the greater good of the state. The concept of rajaniti (king's duty) involves ethical considerations, although pragmatism often outweighs these when it comes to state survival. Machiavelli, on the other hand, is largely unconcerned with traditional moral frameworks. The Prince is often seen as advocating for a complete separation of politics from morality, a significant shift from earlier political theories in the West. For Machiavelli, power and pragmatism are paramount, and moral considerations are secondary to political expediency.

- **Role of the Ruler:** Kautilya sees the ruler as an integral part of society, responsible for ensuring prosperity, justice, and the well-being of subjects. The king has a paternalistic duty to protect and promote the welfare of his people.Machiavelli, while recognizing that the ruler must maintain the support of the people, is more focused on the individual ruler's ability to maintain power. His ruler is often isolated, acting as a shrewd and strategic figure more concerned with power than with the collective good.

- **Scope and Application:** The Artha Shastra is a comprehensive treatise on statecraft, covering not just politics and military strategy, but also economics, social welfare, diplomacy, legal systems, taxation, agriculture, and infrastructure. It offers a more holistic approach to governance.The Prince, by contrast, is more narrowly focused on the art of ruling and the methods a leader should use to maintain and extend his power. Machiavelli doesn't provide a detailed blueprint for governance but concentrates on leadership techniques and the challenges rulers face in a competitive political environment.

- **Philosophical and Religious Context:** The Artha Shastra is embedded in an Indian philosophical context, which includes ideas from Hindu, Buddhist, and Jain traditions. Although Kautilya is pragmatic, he operates within a broader metaphysical framework, acknowledging the role of dharma and the eventual cosmic justice that rulers must consider.Machiavelli is writing during the Renaissance, a time of humanism and secular thought. He largely separates religion from politics, advocating for a form of political pragmatism that doesn't depend on religious or metaphysical beliefs.

- **Ruler's Public Image:** In the Artha Shastra, Kautilya suggests that a ruler should be seen as just, wise, and righteous, even if behind the scenes he employs deception and manipulation. The public image of the ruler as benevolent and ethical is important for maintaining loyalty and order.Machiavelli also acknowledges the importance of a ruler's public image but goes further in emphasizing that a ruler must be willing to project an image of virtue while acting entirely differently if necessary. Machiavelli's ruler is more likely to use fear as a tool for control, while Kautilya tends to balance fear with justice and welfare.

Both Kautilya's Artha Shastra and Machiavelli's The Prince are masterful treatises on power and statecraft, representing sophisticated approaches to ruling in their respective contexts. While both advocate for the pragmatic and sometimes ruthless use of power, their differences lie in their cultural foundations, ethical considerations, and the breadth of their political theories. Kautilya provides a more holistic and socially integrated model of governance, while Machiavelli emphasizes the stark realities of power politics in a more individualized and secular framework.

Contemporary Relevance of Artha Shastra

The principles outlined in the *Artha Shastra* continue to influence modern political thought, particularly in areas such as statecraft, diplomacy, and economic policy. Its emphasis on pragmatism, efficiency, and realpolitik resonates with contemporary political theories of governance and international relations. In India, the text has been revisited as a source of inspiration for modern governance. Many of Kautilya's ideas on taxation, administration, and diplomacy have contemporary relevance in the areas of public administration, economic reforms, and foreign policy.

Conclusion

The *Artha Shastra* remains one of the most comprehensive ancient treatises on governance, economics, and military strategy. Its pragmatic approach to ruling a state, its emphasis on the accumulation of wealth, and its detailed insights into diplomacy and warfare offer timeless lessons for political leaders. While its teachings were intended for the rulers of ancient India, the *Artha Shastra* continues to be studied for its relevance in modern political and economic thought, making it a cornerstone in the global heritage of political philosophy.

Questions for quick revision

1. What is the Artha Shastra, and who is its traditional author?
2. What are the main themes covered in the Artha Shastra?
3. How does the Artha Shastra define the concept of "Artha"?
4. What role does the Artha Shastra play in the context of statecraft and governance?
5. How does the Artha Shastra address economic policies and resource management?
6. What strategies for warfare and diplomacy are discussed in the Artha Shastra?

7. How does the Artha Shastra categorize different types of rulers and their governance styles?

8. In what ways does the Artha Shastra emphasize the importance of intelligence and espionage in governance?

9. How do the principles outlined in the Artha Shastra compare to modern political and economic theories?

10. How has the Artha Shastra influenced contemporary views on politics and economics in India?

CHAPTER FOUR

Natya Shastra: The Ancient Indian Treatise on Performing Arts

The *Natya Shastra* (Sanskrit: नाट्यशास्त्र), attributed to the sage Bharata Muni, is one of the most comprehensive and ancient treatises on the performing arts, encompassing theatre, dance, and music. Written sometime between 200 BCE and 200 CE, this ancient text forms the foundation of Indian classical dance and drama traditions, with its influence extending into modern times. The name *Natya* refers to dramatic arts, while *Shastra* means "science" or "treatise," implying that the text is a scientific and systematic exploration of these art forms. The *Natya Shastra* is not just a manual on how to perform dance and drama but also delves deeply into aesthetics, philosophy, emotions (*rasa*), and the role of art in society. It covers a wide range of topics, including the construction of stages, the training of actors, the intricacies of acting, the classification of musical instruments, and the use of specific body movements and gestures.

This chapter explores the historical significance, structure, major concepts, and contemporary relevance of the *Natya Shastra.*

Historical Context of the Natya Shastra

The *Natya Shastra* was composed during a period of rich cultural development in ancient India, a time when the arts flourished under royal patronage and were deeply interwoven with religion and society. It is said that the treatise was written by the sage Bharata Muni, who was chosen by the gods to create a fifth Veda, called the *Natyaveda,* which would be accessible to all, including those who could not engage with the more ritualistic and philosophical elements of the four Vedas (Rigveda, Samaveda, Yajurveda, and Atharvaveda). This mythical origin story reflects the idea that performance arts, particularly drama, served as a medium for conveying moral and spiritual messages to the masses. The *Natya Shastra* was composed at a time when dance and drama were not just forms of entertainment but integral to religious rites, social life, and education. The *Natya Shastra's* influence extended beyond ancient India, affecting art forms in Southeast Asia, particularly in countries like Cambodia, Thailand, and Indonesia, where Indian classical traditions had spread.

Structure and Content of the Natya Shastra

The *Natya Shastra* consists of 36 chapters (some later versions have as many as 37) and contains approximately 6,000 verses. It provides an encyclopedic account of all aspects of the performing arts, covering everything from dramaturgy to music and dance. The text is highly technical and detailed, providing specific instructions for artists and directors alike.

The main subjects covered in the *Natya Shastra* include:

1. **Origins of Drama and Dance**: The mythological and divine origins of the performing arts.
2. **Construction of Theatres**: Guidelines for building different types of theatres.
3. **Dramatic Performance**: Instructions for staging plays, including the classification of dramatic genres.
4. **Acting (Abhinaya)**: Detailed explanations of different types of acting, including physical gestures, facial expressions, and verbal communication.
5. **Music and Musical Instruments**: Discussions of musical modes, instruments, and how they should accompany drama and dance.
6. **Rasa Theory**: The emotional and aesthetic experience of drama, music, and dance.
7. **Dance Movements**: Detailed analysis of body postures, hand gestures (mudras), footwork, and facial expressions in classical dance.
8. **Costume and Makeup**: Guidelines for costumes, makeup, and the use of masks in performances.

The Divine Origins of Natya: A Sacred form of Art

According to the *Natya Shastra*, drama was created by Brahma, the creator god in Hindu mythology, at the request of the other gods. The gods wanted an art form that was accessible to everyone, regardless of their caste, gender, or education. In response, Brahma combined elements from all four Vedas:

- **Speech** (*pathya*) from the Rigveda,
- **Gesture** (*abhinaya*) from the Yajurveda,
- **Music** (*svara*) from the Samaveda, and
- **Sentiment** (*rasa*) from the Atharvaveda.

Thus, *Natya*, or drama, was seen as a divine creation that encapsulated the essence of all other forms of knowledge and art. Bharata Muni, the sage chosen by Brahma, is considered the first teacher of *Natya* and the one who transmitted this sacred art to humanity. Drama and dance were seen not only as forms of entertainment but also as mediums for moral instruction, spiritual growth, and the promotion of harmony within society. Performances were often staged as part of religious festivals and were imbued with spiritual significance.

The Concept of Rasa: The Essence of Aesthetic Experience

One of the most significant contributions of the *Natya Shastra* is the theory of *Rasa*, which refers to the emotional and aesthetic experience evoked in the audience during a performance. *Rasa* literally means "juice" or "essence," and in the context of the *Natya Shastra*, it denotes the distilled emotional flavor that a drama or dance performance creates in its viewers.

Bharata Muni identifies eight primary *rasas*:

1. **Śṛngāra (Erotic or Romantic)**: The emotion of love, beauty, and attraction.
2. **Hāsya (Humor)**: The feeling of joy and amusement.
3. **Karuṇa (Compassion)**: The feeling of sorrow and empathy.
4. **Raudra (Fury)**: The emotion of anger and wrath.

5. **Vīra (Heroic):** The feeling of valor and courage.
6. **Bhayanaka (Terror):** The emotion of fear and anxiety.
7. **Bībhatsa (Disgust):** The feeling of aversion or repulsion.
8. **Adbhuta (Wonder):** The emotion of surprise and astonishment.

A ninth *rasa* known as **Śānta (Peace)** was added later, representing the feeling of tranquility and contentment. Each of these *rasas* is associated with specific moods (*bhavas*) and is evoked through the performance's combination of acting, music, and dialogue. The primary goal of a performer is to evoke the intended *rasa* in the audience, creating a powerful and transformative emotional experience. The *rasa* theory has had a profound influence on Indian aesthetics and continues to be a central concept in Indian classical dance, theatre, and literature.

Abhinaya: The Art of Acting

Acting, or *abhinaya*, is one of the most important elements of the *Natya Shastra*. Bharata Muni describes *abhinaya* as the expression of the actor's body, gestures, speech, and emotions to communicate the meaning of the performance to the audience. He classifies *abhinaya* into four distinct types:

1. **Āṅgika Abhinaya (Physical Expressions):** This involves the use of the body to convey emotions, including gestures made with the hands (mudras), facial expressions, eye movements, and overall body posture. The *Natya Shastra* provides detailed descriptions of how various parts of the body should be used to communicate different emotions.

2. **Vācika Abhinaya (Verbal Expressions):** This refers to the use of speech, including dialogue, tone, pitch, and pronunciation, to express emotion and meaning. In classical dance forms, this may be expressed through songs or verses that accompany the performance.

3. **Āhārya Abhinaya (Costume and Makeup):** The visual appearance of the performer, including their costumes, makeup, and accessories, contributes to the overall portrayal of the character. These elements help enhance the mood of the performance and define the character's social status, personality, and emotional state.

4. **Sāttvika Abhinaya (Emotional Expressions):** This is the portrayal of subtle, internal emotions, such as a trembling body, teary eyes, or goosebumps. It requires a high level of emotional involvement from the actor and is considered the most difficult form of *abhinaya* to master.

These four types of *abhinaya* work together to evoke the desired *rasa* in the audience. Mastering *abhinaya* requires rigorous training and a deep understanding of the connection between body, mind, and emotions.

Dance and Body Movements in Natya Shastra

The *Natya Shastra* also serves as one of the earliest texts on classical Indian dance. Bharata Muni provides meticulous descriptions of body movements, gestures, and facial expressions that are used to convey meaning in dance performances. The two main types of movements described are:

- **Nritta**: Pure dance movements that are abstract and rhythmical, focusing on the beauty of the movement itself rather than storytelling.
- **Nritya**: Expressive dance movements that communicate a story or emotion through gestures and facial expressions.

In *Nritya*, the *Natya Shastra* describes a wide variety of hand gestures, or *mudras*, each with specific meanings. These gestures are essential for the dancer to communicate with the audience without the use of words. The text outlines:

- **Asamyuta Hastas**: Single-handed gestures, used to represent objects, emotions, or actions.
- **Samyuta Hastas**: Double-handed gestures, often used to represent larger ideas or abstract concepts.

In addition to hand gestures, the text also provides guidance on foot movements (*pada bhedas*), postures (*karanas*), and facial expressions, all of which are integral to classical Indian dance forms such as Bharatanatyam, Kathakali, and Odissi.

Music and Musical Instruments in Natya Shastra

Music plays an essential role in the performance of dance and drama as outlined in the *Natya Shastra*. The text offers detailed discussions on the various musical scales, modes (*ragas*), and rhythmic patterns (*talas*) that accompany dramatic and dance performances. Bharata Muni identifies two main types of music:

1. **Dhruva Gana**: Vocal music that is used to accompany drama, particularly in scenes of heightened emotion or significant action.
2. **Atodya Gana**: Instrumental music, including drums, cymbals, flutes, and string instruments, which adds to the emotional intensity and atmosphere of the performance.

The text also provides classifications of musical instruments into four categories:

- **Tata** (stringed instruments),
- **Avanaddha** (drums),
- **Sushira** (wind instruments), and
- **Ghana** (solid instruments, such as cymbals).

The use of music in the *Natya Shastra* is not merely ornamental; it is essential for enhancing the emotional and aesthetic experience of the audience. The rhythm and melody are carefully crafted to match the mood and pace of the drama or dance being performed.

The Construction of Theatres and Staging

The *Natya Shastra* contains a fascinating and detailed section on the construction of theatres and stages. Bharata Muni offers guidelines for building different types of theatres to suit different kinds of performances. The text describes three main types of theatre layouts:

1. **Rectangular**,
2. **Square**, and
3. **Triangular**.

Each type of theatre has specific dimensions and design elements that ensure optimal acoustics and visibility for the audience. The seating arrangements are also outlined, with specific areas designated for different classes of people. The design of the theatre reflects the inclusive nature of the *Natya Shastra*, as the audience was made up of people from various social backgrounds, and the performances were meant to educate and entertain all members of society.

The Social and Religious Functions of Natya

In ancient Indian society, *Natya* was not only a form of entertainment but also a medium for conveying moral, ethical, and religious teachings. Performances were often staged during religious festivals and were seen as a way to honor the gods and educate the public on issues of righteousness, duty, and social order. The stories depicted in dramas were usually drawn from Hindu epics like the *Mahabharata* and *Ramayana*, as well as from other mythological sources. These performances were a way of reinforcing the values of the time, such as devotion to duty, respect for elders, and the importance of social harmony. Bharata Muni believed that *Natya* had the power to uplift and purify the minds of both performers and spectators, making it a sacred art form that contributed to the well-being of society as a whole.

Contemporary Relevance of Natya Shastra

The *Natya Shastra* continues to have a profound influence on Indian performing arts, particularly in classical dance and theatre. The principles of *rasa*, *abhinaya*, and the use of gestures and music remain central to many forms of Indian classical dance, such as Bharatanatyam, Kathak, Kuchipudi, and Odissi. The text also serves as a foundational reference for modern Indian theatre, and its insights into the emotional and psychological dimensions of performance are studied by actors and directors alike. In addition, the *Natya Shastra*'s holistic approach to the arts, which emphasizes the integration of drama, music, and dance, resonates with contemporary theories of interdisciplinary art forms. Its detailed understanding of human emotions and aesthetics continues to inform not only the performing arts but also modern film, literature, and other creative mediums.

Conclusion

The *Natya Shastra* is one of the most important and comprehensive works on performing arts in the world. Written over two millennia ago, it offers deep insights into the nature of drama, dance, and music, as well as the emotional and psychological impact these art forms have on audiences. Its principles of *rasa* and *abhinaya* continue to shape Indian classical dance and theatre, making it a timeless guide for artists and scholars alike. Through its detailed exploration of performance, aesthetics, and the role of art in society, the *Natya Shastra* transcends its historical context and remains a relevant and powerful text for understanding the emotional and artistic aspects of human experience.

Test Your Knowledge: Practice Questions

1. What is the Natya Shastra, and who is traditionally believed to be its author?
2. In which century was the Natya Shastra written?

3. What are the four primary types of performance arts discussed in the Natya Shastra?

4. What role does the concept of Rasa play in the Natya Shastra?

5. Explain the eight principal Rasa described in the Natya Shastra?

6. What is the significance of Bhava in the context of the Natya Shastra?

7. How does the Natya Shastra define the relationship between the actor and the audience?

8. What the key components of a theatrical performance are as outlined in the Natya Shastra?

9. How does the Natya Shastra influence modern Indian classical dance forms?

10. How has the Natya Shastra been preserved and transmitted through generations in Indian culture?

Vastu Shastra: The Ancient Science of Architecture and Spatial Design

Vastu Shastra (Sanskrit: वास्तुशास्त्र) is an ancient Indian system of architecture and design that focuses on harmonizing the built environment with natural forces to promote health, wealth, and prosperity. Derived from the words "Vastu" (meaning dwelling or building) and "Shastra" (meaning science or doctrine), Vastu Shastra serves as a guide for creating structures that align with cosmic energies. It draws from a blend of art, science, philosophy, and spirituality, recognizing the impact that spatial arrangements, orientations, and natural elements have on human well-being. With origins dating back over 5,000 years, Vastu Shastra was developed in a cultural context where architecture, religion, and cosmology were closely interconnected. This ancient knowledge has influenced many traditional architectural styles in India, and its principles have parallels with other ancient systems such as Feng Shui from China. Today, Vastu Shastra is experiencing a resurgence, with architects, designers, and homeowners alike seeking its wisdom to create balanced, harmonious living spaces.

This chapter delves into the historical context, fundamental principles, guidelines for building construction, symbolism of elements, and the contemporary relevance of Vastu Shastra.

Historical Background and Origins of Vastu Shastra

The origins of Vastu Shastra can be traced back to the Vedic period, where references to the principles of spatial design appear in texts like the *Rigveda* and *Atharvaveda*. Later, classical texts such as the *Manasara* and *Mayamata* offered more formalized versions of Vastu knowledge. The creation of temples, homes, and even cities in ancient India was guided by the principles outlined in these texts. Vastu Shastra evolved during a time when architecture was deeply interwoven with religious rituals and cosmology. It was believed that the physical environment influenced spiritual well-being, and that creating harmonious structures could enhance one's relationship with the cosmos. The science of Vastu was closely tied to Hindu temple architecture, as temples were designed to reflect the cosmic order, with their layout symbolizing the divine connection between heaven and earth.

Notable historical examples of Vastu-compliant architecture include ancient cities such as Mohenjo-Daro and Harappa from the Indus Valley Civilization, which exhibit systematic layouts and grid-like plans that are consistent with Vastu principles. Over time, Vastu Shastra evolved into a comprehensive architectural system used for designing residential buildings, temples, palaces, and entire cities.

The Cosmic Foundation of Vastu: Purusha Mandala

At the core of Vastu Shastra is the concept of the *Purusha Mandala*, a sacred geometric diagram that represents the cosmic being (Purusha) and the divine order of the universe. The Mandala is a square divided into a grid, typically consisting of 64 or 81 smaller squares, with each square representing a particular deity or cosmic force. The center of the Mandala, known as the *Brahmasthan*, is considered the most sacred space, symbolizing the connection between the human and the divine. The *Purusha Mandala* serves as the template for the layout of buildings and cities in Vastu Shastra. The orientation, dimensions, and placement of structures within this grid are intended to harmonize the flow of cosmic energy (*prana*) in a way that promotes balance and well-being. It is believed that the proper alignment of the Purusha Mandala with the cardinal directions channels positive energy into the space, while any misalignment can lead to negative effects such as ill health, financial loss, or disharmony.

This focus on cosmic alignment is why Vastu emphasizes the importance of directionality in architecture, which leads to the careful selection of building orientations based on the cardinal directions (north, south, east, and west) and the positions of celestial bodies like the sun, moon, and planets.

Five Elements (Pancha Mahabhutas) in Vastu Shastra

One of the fundamental principles of Vastu Shastra is the harmonious integration of the five great elements (*Pancha Mahabhutas*), which are believed to be the building blocks of the universe. These elements are:

1. **Earth (Prithvi)**: Represents stability and grounding. The direction associated with earth is the southwest.
2. **Water (Jal)**: Symbolizes flow, purity, and life. The direction associated with water is the northeast.
3. **Fire (Agni)**: Denotes energy, passion, and transformation. The direction associated with fire is the southeast.
4. **Air (Vayu)**: Stands for movement, freedom, and growth. The direction associated with air is the northwest.
5. **Space (Akasha)**: Represents the infinite and the etheric. The central space of a building is associated with *Akasha*.

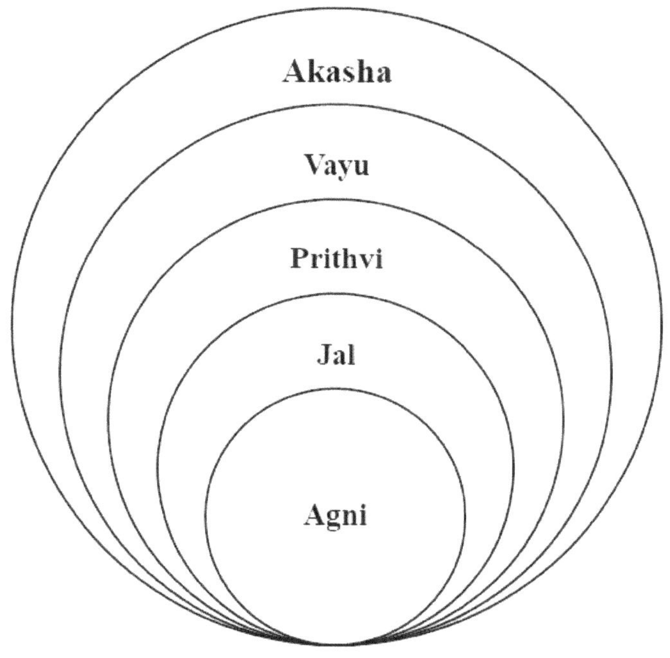

Pancha Mahabhutas in Vastu Shastra Caption

Vastu Shastra seeks to create a balance between these five elements in the built environment. For example, water sources such as wells or ponds are traditionally placed in the northeast corner of a property to capture the beneficial energies associated with that direction, while fire-related activities, such as cooking, are located in the southeast to align with the natural power of the fire element. A well-designed Vastu home or building ensures that these elements are in equilibrium, contributing to the overall health and prosperity of its inhabitants.

Directions and Their Significance in Vastu Shastra

In Vastu Shastra, directions are of paramount importance. The orientation of a building determines how it interacts with the natural forces and cosmic energies. Each direction is ruled by specific deities and associated with particular qualities:

- **East (Purva)**: Ruled by the Sun God, Surya, the east is associated with vitality, new beginnings, and prosperity. It is considered auspicious to have the main entrance facing east to invite the energy of growth and success.
- **West (Paschima)**: Ruled by Varuna, the god of water, the west is linked to stability and support. However, too much emphasis on the west can result in lethargy and stagnation.
- **North (Uttara)**: Ruled by Kubera, the god of wealth, the north is associated with prosperity and financial gain. Having the main entrance or placing valuables in the northern part of the house is considered beneficial for accumulating wealth.
- **South (Dakshina)**: Ruled by Yama, the god of death, the south is associated with discipline, strength, and detachment. While it is not considered inauspicious, care should be taken when designing structures that face south to avoid negative energy.

The *Brahmasthan*, or the center of a Vastu structure, is left open or free of obstructions to allow cosmic energy to flow unimpeded. This central area represents the heart of the space and should remain uncluttered to ensure a positive environment.

Guidelines for Residential Architecture in Vastu Shastra

The application of Vastu Shastra in the design and layout of residential buildings is aimed at promoting harmony, prosperity, and well-being for the inhabitants. Specific guidelines are provided for the placement of different rooms and functions within the house to ensure the optimal flow of energy.

1. **Main Entrance**: The main door is considered the gateway for energy to enter the home. An east or north-facing entrance is preferred, as these directions are associated with positive energy, growth, and prosperity.
2. **Living Room**: The living room should be located in the northeast, north, or east part of the house. This ensures that it is exposed to natural light and air, creating a welcoming and vibrant space for family gatherings.
3. **Kitchen**: The kitchen is ideally located in the southeast, the direction ruled by Agni (fire). If the southeast is not available, the northwest is an alternative option. The cook should face east while preparing food, as this direction is linked to good health and energy.
4. **Bedrooms**: The master bedroom should be located in the southwest, the most stable direction, which is associated with grounding and strength. Children's bedrooms can be placed in the west or northwest, promoting growth and independence.
5. **Bathrooms**: The ideal location for bathrooms is in the northwest or southeast, where the energies of air and fire can facilitate cleanliness and hygiene.

6. **Staircases**: Staircases should ascend clockwise and be located in the south, west, or southwest areas of the house. Improper placement of staircases can lead to financial instability and health problems.

7. **Pooja Room (Prayer Room)**: The northeast, or *Ishanya* corner, is considered the most auspicious location for a pooja room, as it is associated with the element of water and is considered the space closest to divine energies.

Temple Architecture and Vastu Shastra

Vastu Shastra plays a crucial role in the design and construction of Hindu temples, where the principles of cosmic alignment and spiritual symbolism are intricately woven into the structure. Temples are not just places of worship but also physical representations of the cosmos, designed to channel divine energy to the worshippers.

The layout of a temple follows the principles of the *Purusha Mandala*, with the sanctum sanctorum (*garbhagriha*) located at the center of the Mandala, representing the innermost space of the cosmic being. The spire (*shikhara*) above the sanctum is designed to symbolize the connection between earth and the heavens, reaching towards the divine. The placement of deities within the temple is also carefully guided by Vastu principles, with different gods and goddesses occupying specific directions based on their cosmic associations. The entire structure is meant to serve as a microcosm of the universe, creating a space where devotees can engage in spiritual practices and experience divine energies.

The Role of Colors and Materials in Vastu Shastra

Vastu Shastra also provides guidance on the use of colors and materials in building design, as these elements are believed to have an impact on the energy and atmosphere of the space. Different colors are associated with different directions and elements, and their appropriate use can enhance the positive energy in the building:

- **White**: Associated with purity and the element of space, white is often used in the northeast and center of the house to create a calm and harmonious atmosphere.
- **Yellow**: Symbolizing knowledge and wisdom, yellow is suitable for study rooms and libraries, particularly in the west or northeast areas.
- **Red and Orange**: Linked to the fire element, red and orange can be used in the kitchen or southeast areas to enhance vitality and energy.
- **Green**: Representing growth and prosperity, green is ideal for the north or east areas, particularly in rooms where creativity and focus are needed.

Vastu Shastra and Urban Planning

Vastu Shastra is not limited to the design of individual buildings but also extends to urban planning. Ancient Indian cities were often designed based on Vastu principles, with the layout of streets, public buildings, and markets carefully aligned with the cardinal directions and cosmic forces. The city of Jaipur, for instance, is a well-known example of Vastu-compliant urban planning.

Designed in the 18th century by Maharaja Sawai Jai Singh II, Jaipur's grid-like layout follows the principles of the *Purusha Mandala*, with important buildings and public spaces positioned in alignment with cosmic forces. The city's wide streets, public squares, and royal palaces all reflect the harmonious integration of architecture and natural energy.

Contemporary Relevance of Vastu Shastra

In modern times, the principles of Vastu Shastra continue to be applied in residential and commercial architecture, as well as urban planning. As interest in holistic and sustainable living grows, many people are turning to Vastu to create environments that promote health, prosperity, and well-being. While modern architects may not always follow Vastu principles to the letter, many incorporate its guidelines into their designs, particularly with regard to the orientation of buildings, the use of natural light, and the balance of the five elements. In addition, the rising popularity of green architecture and sustainable design aligns with Vastu's emphasis on harmony with nature.

Conclusion

Vastu Shastra, the ancient science of architecture and spatial design, remains a valuable source of wisdom for creating harmonious living environments. Its holistic approach, which integrates the elements of nature, cosmic forces, and human needs, offers timeless insights into the relationship between space and well-being. Whether in the design of homes, temples, or entire cities, Vastu Shastra continues to inspire architects and homeowners to create spaces that not only meet functional needs but also promote physical, mental, and spiritual health.

Questions for Review

1. What is Vastu Shastra, and what is its primary purpose?
2. What are the five elements (Pancha Mahabhutas) considered in Vastu Shastra?
3. How does Vastu Shastra influence the design and construction of buildings?
4. What is the importance of the four cardinal directions in Vastu Shastra?
5. What are the guidelines for the placement of the main entrance of a house according to Vastu Shastra?
6. How does Vastu Shastra suggest positioning rooms like the kitchen, bedroom, and bathroom in a house?
7. What are the benefits of following Vastu principles in modern architecture?
8. How does Vastu Shastra address the importance of natural light and ventilation in buildings?
9. What is the role of water bodies and their placement according to Vastu Shastra?
10. How does Vastu Shastra relate to modern sustainability and eco-friendly architecture?

CHAPTER SIX

Jyotisha Shastra: The Ancient Indian Science of Astrology and Astronomy

Jyotisha Shastra (Sanskrit: ज्योतिषि शास्त्र) is the ancient Indian system of astrology and astronomy, a key component of the Vedic sciences. The term *Jyotisha* is derived from the Sanskrit word "Jyoti," which means light or illumination, signifying its function as a guiding light to understanding cosmic patterns and their influence on human life. As one of the six Vedangas (auxiliary disciplines related to the Vedas), Jyotisha Shastra deals with the observation and calculation of celestial phenomena and their correlation with earthly events. Its application ranges from personal horoscopes to agricultural planning and the timing of rituals. Jyotisha has evolved over thousands of years, intertwining mathematical precision with spiritual insight. In traditional Indian culture, astrology is considered a sacred art that provides individuals with guidance regarding life events, while astronomy contributes to an understanding of cosmic order and timekeeping. The Shastra serves as both a metaphysical tool to decipher karma and fate and a scientific system to calculate the movement of celestial bodies.

This chapter explores the origins of Jyotisha Shastra, its core principles, divisions, the role of horoscopes, and its continued relevance in contemporary times.

Origins and Historical Development of Jyotisha Shastra

Jyotisha Shastra has its roots in the Vedic period, dating back to at least 1500 BCE, when early Indian astronomers and astrologers studied celestial patterns to aid in religious practices and seasonal events. Some of the earliest references to Jyotisha can be found in the Vedic texts, particularly in the *Rigveda* and *Yajurveda*, which contain hymns related to the observation of the sun, moon, and stars. However, it was the *Vedanga Jyotisha*, a specific treatise on astronomy and astrology that formalized the system. Written around 1200 BCE, this text focused on timekeeping for religious ceremonies and described methods for calculating planetary positions and the phases of the moon. These calculations were critical for determining the auspicious timing (*muhurtas*) of rituals, sacrifices, and festivals.

The science of Jyotisha continued to develop over centuries, with contributions from notable scholars such as Aryabhata, Varahamihira, and Bhaskara II. Varahamihira's *Brihat Samhita*, written in the 6th century CE, was a seminal text that dealt with a wide range of astrological topics, from planetary movements to weather forecasting. Throughout

Indian history, Jyotisha remained integral to not just religious life but also statecraft. Kings consulted astrologers to determine the best times for wars, alliances, and administrative decisions. Astrology was also closely linked to Ayurvedic medicine, as a person's astrological chart (or *kundali*) was often consulted to diagnose and treat illnesses.

The Philosophical Foundations of Jyotisha Shastra

At the heart of Jyotisha Shastra is the belief in the interconnectedness of the cosmos and human life. This concept is rooted in the doctrine of *karma* (actions and their consequences) and *samsara* (the cycle of birth, death, and rebirth), which form the spiritual foundation of Hindu philosophy. According to Jyotisha, celestial bodies like the sun, moon, planets, and stars are not merely distant physical entities but also manifestations of divine energy that exert subtle influences on human destiny. The movements of these bodies are seen as indicators of karmic patterns that affect individuals, societies, and the natural world.

Time, as conceived in Jyotisha, is cyclical, with planetary movements reflecting the eternal rhythms of creation, preservation, and dissolution. The astrological chart serves as a map of these rhythms, helping individuals understand the cosmic forces that shape their lives. Unlike the fatalistic interpretations often associated with astrology in the West, Jyotisha emphasizes that while planetary influences can shape circumstances, human effort (*purushartha*) and free will can modify outcomes. Astrology in this context is a tool for self-awareness and spiritual growth.

Divisions of Jyotisha Shastra: Siddhanta, Samhita, and Hora

Jyotisha Shastra is traditionally divided into three main branches:

1. **Siddhanta (Astronomy)**: This branch deals with mathematical astronomy and the scientific study of planetary positions, lunar and solar eclipses, and time measurement. Siddhanta forms the foundation of Jyotisha, as accurate astronomical calculations are necessary for astrological predictions. Texts like Aryabhata's *Aryabhatiya* and Bhaskara II's *Siddhanta Shiromani* are key works in this field. In modern terms, Siddhanta can be compared to the field of astrophysics.

2. **Samhita (Mundane Astrology)**: Samhita is the branch of Jyotisha that focuses on mundane astrology, which is concerned with collective events like weather patterns, natural disasters, wars, and political developments. Samhita also encompasses *Vaastu Shastra* (the science of architecture) and *Muhurtashastra* (the science of auspicious timings). Varahamihira's *Brihat Samhita* is a classic example of a text that covers various aspects of Samhita, including omens and portents.

3. **Hora (Predictive Astrology)**: The most commonly known aspect of Jyotisha, Hora deals with individual astrology and is used to predict personal events based on the positions of the planets at the time of a person's birth. This branch is where the *kundali* or birth chart comes into play. It includes the interpretation of planetary transits, *dashas* (planetary periods), and *yogas* (planetary combinations) to understand life's trajectory.

Each branch of Jyotisha serves a distinct purpose but is interconnected with the others, allowing for a holistic understanding of cosmic influences on both personal and collective levels.

The Twelve Houses and Their Significance

In Hora or predictive astrology, the birth chart is divided into twelve houses (*bhavas*), each representing a different aspect of life. These houses are analogous to areas of human experience, such as relationships, career, and health. The positioning of planets in these houses at the time of birth influences the individual's characteristics, life events, and challenges. Here is a brief overview of the twelve houses in Jyotisha:

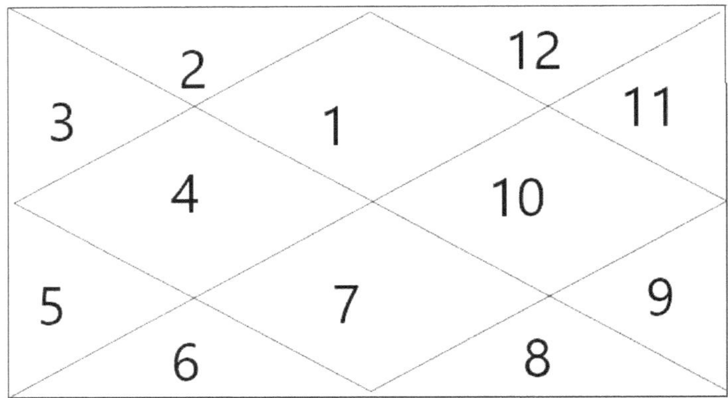

Representation of twelve houses in a horoscope

1. **First House (Lagna/Bhava)**: Represents the self, physical appearance, and personality.

2. **Second House**: Deals with wealth, speech, family, and accumulated possessions.
3. **Third House**: Represents courage, siblings, communication, and short journeys.
4. **Fourth House**: Associated with home, mother, property, and emotional well-being.
5. **Fifth House**: Governs intelligence, children, creativity, and romantic relationships.
6. **Sixth House**: Linked to health, enemies, obstacles, and service.
7. **Seventh House**: Represents marriage, partnerships, and business ventures.
8. **Eighth House**: Concerns transformation, death, inheritance, and occult knowledge.
9. **Ninth House**: Associated with higher learning, spirituality, long journeys, and luck.
10. **Tenth House**: Governs career, reputation, and public life.
11. **Eleventh House**: Represents gains, social circles, and aspirations.
12. **Twelfth House**: Concerns loss, expenditure, isolation, and spiritual liberation.

The planets occupying these houses, as well as their aspects and conjunctions, determine how these areas of life manifest for the individual.

The Nine Planets (Navagrahas) in Jyotisha Shastra

Jyotisha Shastra identifies nine primary celestial bodies, known as the *Navagrahas* (nine planets), which play a crucial role in astrological interpretations. These include seven visible planets from traditional astronomy and two shadowy planets, Rahu and Ketu, which represent the lunar nodes.

1. **Surya (Sun)**: The Sun represents the soul, ego, vitality, and authority. Its position in the chart indicates one's sense of self and leadership qualities.
2. **Chandra (Moon)**: The Moon governs the mind, emotions, and intuition. Its placement affects mental stability, emotional responses, and maternal influence.
3. **Mangal (Mars)**: Mars signifies energy, action, and aggression. It is associated with courage, ambition, and conflict.
4. **Budh (Mercury)**: Mercury represents intellect, communication, and adaptability. It influences skills in writing, speaking, and commerce.
5. **Guru (Jupiter)**: Jupiter is the planet of wisdom, expansion, and benevolence. It governs spiritual growth, education, and wealth.
6. **Shukra (Venus)**: Venus is associated with love, beauty, art, and relationships. Its influence extends to sensuality, luxury, and creativity.
7. **Shani (Saturn)**: Saturn symbolizes discipline, responsibility, and hardship. It governs time, karma, and life lessons, often bringing challenges that lead to personal growth.
8. **Rahu**: Rahu represents obsession, confusion, and material desire. As a shadow planet, it creates illusions and brings unorthodox approaches to life.
9. **Ketu**: Ketu signifies detachment, spirituality, and past-life karma. It brings mystical experiences and spiritual enlightenment but also challenges related to material life.

The positions and movements of these planets, their aspects, and their relationships with each other form the basis for astrological readings in Jyotisha. Table below represents nine planets from Vedic Astrology and their influence on the buman body

Sr. No.	Name of Planet	Influence on human body
1	Sun (Surya)	Governs the **heart**, circulatory system, and overall vitality. Represents the soul and consciousness.
2	Moon (Chandra)	Governs the mind, emotions, fluids in the body, and sleep patterns
3	Mars (Mangal)	Influences blood, muscles, and energy. Associated with strength, courage, and determination.
4	Mercury (Budh)	Governs the nervous system, skin, and intellect. Associated with communication and reasoning.
5	Jupiter (Guru)	Influences the liver, growth, and fat tissues. Represents wisdom, knowledge, and expansion.
6	Venus (Shukra)	Governs the reproductive system, kidneys, and artistic pursuits. Represents love, beauty, and pleasure.
7	Saturn (Shani)	Affects the bones, teeth, and skin. Represents discipline, structure, and limitations.
8	Rahu	Governs desires, obsessions, and psychological issues. Represents illusion and worldly ambitions.
9	Ketu	Influences spirituality and detachment, particularly the feet. Represents past karma and liberation.

Rashis (zodiac signs)

In Vedic astrology (Jyotish), the 12 Rashis (zodiac signs) hold significant importance as they represent various personality traits, characteristics, and life experiences. Each sign corresponds to 30 degrees of the celestial circle and has a ruling planet, an element, and other associations. Here's a detailed look at the 12 Rashis and their significance:

1. **Mesha (Aries) - मेष**

- Symbol: Sheep
- Ruling Planet: Mars (Mangal)
- Element: Fire
- Quality: Cardinal

Significance: People born under Mesha are known for their courage, initiative, leadership qualities, and dynamic personality. They are energetic, adventurous, and like to take risks but can be impulsive and quick-tempered.

2. **Vrishabha (Taurus) - वृषभ**

- Symbol: Bull
- Ruling Planet: Venus (Shukra)
- Element: Earth
- Quality: Fixed

Significance: Vrishabha individuals are steady, reliable, and patient. They value comfort, beauty, and stability. They are materialistic but also grounded, with a strong sense of practicality. Their stubbornness, however, can make them inflexible.

3. **Mithuna (Gemini) - मिथुन**

- Symbol: Twins
- Ruling Planet: Mercury (Budh)
- Element: Air
- Quality: Mutable

Significance: Those born under Mithuna are curious, adaptable, and communicative. They have an intellectual mindset and are quick-witted, but they can also be inconsistent and indecisive due to their dual nature.

4. Karka (Cancer) - कर्क

- Symbol: Crab
- Ruling Planet: Moon (Chandra)
- Element: Water
- Quality: Cardinal

Significance: Karka people are emotional, nurturing, and protective. They are highly intuitive and sensitive to their surroundings. They are compassionate but can also be moody and overly attached to their past.

5. Simha (Leo) - सिंह

- Symbol: Lion
- Ruling Planet: Sun (Surya)
- Element: Fire
- Quality: Fixed

Significance: Simha individuals are charismatic, confident, and natural-born leaders. They possess a regal bearing and take pride in their achievements. They can, however, be egoistic and crave attention or admiration.

6. Kanya (Virgo) - कन्या

- Symbol: Virgin

- Ruling Planet: Mercury (Budh)
- Element: Earth
- Quality: Mutable

Significance: People born under Kanya are analytical, detail-oriented, and organized. They are perfectionists who thrive on order and precision but can sometimes be overly critical and worry too much about minor details.

7. Tula (Libra) - तुला

- Symbol: Scales
- Ruling Planet: Venus (Shukra)
- Element: Air
- Quality: Cardinal

Significance: Tula individuals value balance, harmony, and fairness. They are diplomatic and charming, often seeking peace in their relationships. However, they may have difficulty making decisions due to their desire to weigh all options.

8. Vrishchika (Scorpio) - वृश्चकि

- Symbol: Scorpion
- Ruling Planet: Mars (Mangal), Ketu (Co-ruler in some interpretations)
- Element: Water
- Quality: Fixed

Significance: Vrishchika natives are intense, passionate, and determined. They are secretive, resourceful, and often magnetic in their personal power. Their deep emotions can lead them to be possessive and sometimes vengeful.

9. Dhanu (Sagittarius) - धनु

- Symbol: Archer
- Ruling Planet: Jupiter (Guru)
- Element: Fire
- Quality: Mutable

Significance: Dhanu individuals are optimistic, philosophical, and freedom-loving. They are adventurous, with a love for travel and new experiences. They can, however, be overly idealistic or tactless in their pursuit of truth.

10. Makara (Capricorn) - मकर

- Symbol: Sea Goat
- Ruling Planet: Saturn (Shani)
- Element: Earth
- Quality: Cardinal

Significance: Makara natives are disciplined, responsible, and practical. They value hard work and long-term achievements. They can be ambitious but also may come across as cold or overly focused on material success.

11. Kumbha (Aquarius) - कुम्भ

- Symbol: Water Bearer

- Ruling Planet: Saturn (Shani), Rahu (Co-ruler in some interpretations)
- Element: Air
- Quality: Fixed

Significance: Kumbha individuals are innovative, humanitarian, and forward-thinking. They have a unique and unconventional outlook on life. They are friendly but may also be detached or eccentric in their approach to relationships.

12. **Meena (Pisces) - मीन**

- Symbol: Fishes
- Ruling Planet: Jupiter (Guru)
- Element: Water
- Quality: Mutable

Significance: Meena people are empathetic, artistic, and deeply spiritual. They are dreamers with a strong sense of intuition, often drawn to mystical or imaginative pursuits. However, they can also be escapist or overly idealistic.

Relevance of the 12 Rashis in Vedic Astrology

CHAPTER SEVEN

Shilpa Shastra: The Science of Art and Craft in Ancient India

Shilpa Shastra (शिल्प शास्त्र) is an ancient Indian text that deals with the principles of art, architecture, sculpture, and craftsmanship. The term "Shilpa" refers to art or craftsmanship, while "Shastra" means a body of knowledge or science. Thus, Shilpa Shastra can be understood as the "science of art." It encompasses a vast range of subjects including sculpture, iconography, temple architecture, and fine arts such as painting and jewelry design. Derived from the Sanskrit word "Shilpa" meaning craft or art, and "Shastra" meaning science, Shilpa Shastra forms an essential component of the broader Vedic knowledge system, blending artistic expression with spiritual and architectural principles. Its scope ranges from the design of temples and idols to traditional handicrafts, sculptures, and aesthetic forms. Shilpa Shastra integrates aesthetics with the metaphysical, blending form and function in an inseparable relationship between art and spirituality. The central philosophy behind Shilpa Shastra is that art and architecture are not merely decorative but serve as mediums to express divine principles and cosmic order.

This chapter delves into the origins, guiding principles, forms, and applications of Shilpa Shastra, with an emphasis on how it influenced Indian art, architecture, and cultural expressions across history.

Historical Background

Shilpa Shastra is deeply rooted in the Vedic tradition, drawing its philosophical foundation from the Vedas, Upanishads, and Puranas. Early references to Shilpa Shastra can be traced to ancient texts like the Rig Veda, which speaks of the creative process and craftsmanship involved in the creation of sacred objects and spaces. Over time, the knowledge evolved into specialized treatises that detailed the principles of architecture and sculpture.

Key texts in the development of Shilpa Shastra include the Vishwakarma Shilpa Shastra, Manasara Shilpa Shastra, and Mayamatam. These texts, named after mythological and divine architects like Vishwakarma and Maya, provided rules for creating temples, idols, and other forms of sacred art. Vishwakarma is traditionally regarded as the divine architect and craftsman, and much of the early knowledge related to Shilpa Shastra is ascribed to him and his followers. Shilpa Shastra reached its pinnacle during the Gupta period (4th–6th centuries CE), when temple architecture, sculpture, and iconography flourished. This era saw a refinement in the principles of proportion, symmetry, and aesthetics in creating sacred and civic spaces. Several texts contribute to the body of Shilpa Shastra, including:

- **Manasara Shilpa Shastra**: An authoritative text on architecture and sculpture.
- **Samarangana Sutradhara**: Written by King Bhoja, it discusses various aspects of art and architecture.
- **Vishwakarma Prakash**: A comprehensive treatise on architecture and sculpture.

Guiding Principles of Shilpa Shastra

Shilpa Shastra is governed by a series of guiding principles that emphasize harmony, balance, and spiritual alignment. These principles are not restricted to physical aesthetics but also focus on metaphysical concerns, ensuring that every structure or artwork serves a higher spiritual purpose.

- Proportion (Tala): Proportion is one of the fundamental aspects of Shilpa Shastra. Whether in the design of temples, sculptures, or paintings, specific ratios known as tala must be followed to maintain balance and symmetry. For example, the measurements of a deity's idol or a temple's structure are based on precise ratios that align with cosmological and human scales. These proportions are said to reflect the harmony of the universe and the human body, considered a microcosm of the cosmos.
- Symmetry (Samya): Symmetry, both bilateral and radial, plays a crucial role in Shilpa Shastra. In temple architecture, for instance, the layout is often symmetrical along central axes, ensuring a harmonious visual experience. This symmetry also extends to sculptural art, where each feature of the deity or

structure is carefully balanced to reflect a divine order.

- Orientation (Dik): The orientation of temples, idols, and other structures is dictated by cosmic principles. Temples are typically aligned with the cardinal directions, with the main entrance often facing east to welcome the rising sun. This alignment is symbolic of the connection between the material world and the divine.

- Material Selection (Dravya): Shilpa Shastra provides detailed guidance on the selection of materials for construction and art. Different materials such as stone, wood, metal, and clay are used depending on the type of structure or artwork. The choice of material is closely related to the intended spiritual purpose, and certain materials are believed to have specific energies or symbolic meanings.

- Rasa (Aesthetic Flavor): Aesthetic experience is an integral part of Shilpa Shastra. The concept of rasa, or aesthetic flavor, pertains to the emotions and spiritual states evoked by a piece of art. In temple design and iconography, the rasa experienced by devotees contributes to the emotional and spiritual upliftment, enabling a direct connection with the divine. Sculptures, for example, aim to evoke emotions such as peace, devotion, or awe.

Architectural Traditions in Shilpa Shastra

Shilpa Shastra outlines the principles of architecture, particularly focusing on sacred structures like temples, palaces, and other religious or civic buildings. These architectural traditions are seen as ways to connect the earthly and divine realms, with temples serving as earthly abodes for deities. Temple Architecture: Temple design is one of the most significant aspects of Shilpa Shastra. The temple is viewed as a microcosm of the universe, with every element—from the foundation to the spire—symbolizing various cosmic principles. The layout of a Hindu temple is based on a mandala (a geometric diagram), which ensures the alignment of the temple with the cosmic order.

Temples are divided into three main parts:

- **Garbhagriha (Sanctum Sanctorum):** The innermost chamber of the temple where the main deity is enshrined. This part of the temple is usually dark and intimate, representing the womb of creation.
- **Mandapa (Pillared Hall):** A hall where devotees gather for prayers or rituals. This space is often richly decorated with carvings, signifying the transition from the material world to the divine.
- **Shikhara (Tower or Spire):** The towering structure above the garbhagriha symbolizing Mount Meru, the axis of the universe. The height and design of the shikhara are guided by Vedic principles, representing the spiritual ascent.

The architectural styles of temples vary across India, with major traditions including:

- **Nagara Style (North Indian temples):** Characterized by a beehive-shaped shikhara and minimalistic exterior.
- **Dravida Style (South Indian temples):** Known for its pyramid-like vimana and elaborately carved gopurams (gateway towers).

- **Vesara Style:** A hybrid of Nagara and Dravida styles, found in central India.
- **Palaces and Secular Architecture:** While Shilpa Shastra primarily deals with religious structures, it also provides guidelines for the design of royal palaces and other civic structures. Palaces were designed with the same attention to proportions, symmetry, and cosmic alignment as temples, often serving as symbols of the king's divine right to rule.

Sculpture and Iconography in Shilpa Shastra

Shilpa Shastra extensively deals with the creation of sculptures and icons, particularly for religious purposes. The figures of deities, humans, and mythological beings are crafted based on specific guidelines that focus on proportion, expression, and symbolism.

- Idol Creation (Pratima Lakshana): The creation of idols is governed by precise rules, known as pratima lakshana. Sculptors are required to follow measurements and proportions outlined in the Shilpa Shastra texts to ensure the divine presence in the idol. Each part of the deity's body, from the posture to the facial expressions, holds symbolic meaning. For example:
- Mudras (hand gestures): These are essential in conveying the deity's role, such as protection, blessing, or teaching.
- Attributes: The weapons, ornaments, and symbols held by deities (like Vishnu's conch or Shiva's trident) are carefully defined to communicate specific spiritual meanings.

- Human and Animal Sculpture: Besides religious icons, Shilpa Shastra also outlines guidelines for human and animal sculptures. These sculptures, used in both secular and religious contexts, must adhere to principles of balance, movement, and expression.
- Relief Sculptures and Carvings: Temples and palaces were often adorned with intricate relief carvings that depicted mythological scenes, stories from the epics, and various deities. These carvings were not merely decorative but served as teaching tools for devotees, illustrating spiritual narratives and principles.

Painting, Handicrafts, and Fine Arts

In addition to architecture and sculpture, Shilpa Shastra also encompasses other forms of art, including painting, handicrafts, and textile design.

Painting (Chitra Karma): Painting, known as chitra karma, is another important aspect of Shilpa Shastra. The treatises provide rules for painting styles, colors, and subject matter. Paintings often depict religious themes, including scenes from Hindu mythology, but also feature secular subjects like royal life and nature. The choice of colors and forms is meant to evoke specific rasa (emotional responses) and align with spiritual themes.

Handicrafts: Traditional Indian handicrafts, from pottery to metalwork and jewelry design, are also governed by Shilpa Shastra principles. Artisans are expected to maintain aesthetic balance, harmony, and adherence to symbolic meanings in their work. These crafts serve not only functional purposes but also reflect spiritual and cultural values.

Influence and Legacy of Shilpa Shastra

Shilpa Shastra's influence extends beyond India, with elements of its principles being adopted in neighbouring countries such as Cambodia, Thailand, and Indonesia, especially in temple architecture and sculpture. The legacy of Shilpa Shastra can be seen in the grand temples of Angkor Wat, the Borobudur stupa, and various Southeast Asian monuments. In modern India, Shilpa Shastra continues to inspire contemporary architecture, sculpture, and art. Many traditional artisans still refer to these ancient texts for guidance, preserving the knowledge and techniques passed down through generations.

Significance of Shilpa Shastra

Cultural Importance

The cultural importance of Shilpa Shastra lies in its profound impact on the development of Indian art, architecture, and craft traditions. As an ancient and comprehensive treatise on arts and crafts, it played a pivotal role in shaping not only the physical environment of India—through its guidelines for temple construction, sculpture, and iconography—but also the spiritual, aesthetic, and social fabric of Indian society. Shilpa Shastra is intricately linked to the religious and spiritual traditions of India, particularly Hinduism, Buddhism, and Jainism. It provides the technical and symbolic framework for creating religious monuments, sacred sculptures, and spaces of worship. By following the principles of Shilpa Shastra, artists and architects created temples, idols, and symbols that were not merely aesthetically pleasing but also infused with spiritual meaning. Temples built according to Shilpa Shastra principles were designed to symbolize the cosmos. The central sanctum (garbhagriha) represented the divine womb, while the spire (shikhara) symbolized the axis mundi, or the connection between heaven and earth. These architectural elements facilitated spiritual practices, helping devotees align themselves with the universe and their deity. Shilpa Shastra defined the rules for crafting religious icons and deities, ensuring that each element, posture, and hand gesture (mudra) was symbolic. These idols were not merely representations but were believed to house the deity's spirit, making them central to religious rituals and worship practices.

Preservation of Traditional Knowledge and Craftsmanship

Shilpa Shastra played a key role in preserving India's rich tradition of craftsmanship, passing down knowledge of sculpting, architecture, painting, and metalwork from one generation to the next. This continuity of skill and knowledge has helped preserve India's diverse artistic heritage, allowing it to flourish over centuries.

Influence on Indian Architecture and Urban Planning

Shilpa Shastra's guidelines extended to urban planning and public works, influencing the layout of cities, palaces, and civic buildings. The principles of symmetry, spatial arrangement, and alignment with natural elements like sunlight and wind were applied not only to religious structures but also to towns and cities. Shilpa Shastra includes principles of Vastu Shastra, which governs the spatial arrangement of buildings to create harmony between humans and nature. This ensured that cities and towns were laid out in a way that promoted prosperity, health, and well-being.

Aesthetic and Artistic Influence

Shilpa Shastra's detailed guidelines on proportions, symmetry, and the use of space have had a lasting impact on Indian aesthetics. The treatise outlines how different art forms, including sculpture, painting, and decoration, should be created to evoke specific emotional responses (rasa). It emphasizes the importance of evoking particular emotions in viewers through the creation of art. Whether it is a temple sculpture meant to inspire devotion or a painting designed to evoke tranquillity, the principles of Shilpa Shastra ensure that art is both functional and emotionally resonant.

Cultural Identity and National Heritage

Shilpa Shastra has played an essential role in defining and preserving India's cultural identity. Through its influence on temple design, sculpture, and art, Shilpa Shastra has left an indelible mark on Indian culture, creating a shared aesthetic and spiritual framework that continues to resonate today. Many of India's most celebrated monuments, which are recognized as UNESCO World Heritage Sites, were constructed using the principles of Shilpa Shastra. These include the Sun Temple at Konark, the Brihadeeswarar Temple at Thanjavur, and the Mahabalipuram monuments. These structures not only embody India's cultural heritage but also attract millions of visitors, both from within India and abroad, thereby strengthening India's global cultural presence. The principles of Shilpa Shastra are also evident in the design of temporary structures used during festivals, such as the grand pandals created during Durga Puja in West Bengal or Ganesh Chaturthi in Maharashtra. These temporary yet intricately designed structures showcase the continued relevance of Shilpa Shastra in contemporary cultural practices.

Influence beyond India

Cross-Cultural Exchange: In contemporary India, there is a growing movement to revive the principles of Shilpa Shastra, particularly in the field of architecture and traditional crafts. As India modernizes, there is an increasing awareness of the need to preserve its cultural heritage while incorporating traditional principles into modern design and construction. The principles of Shilpa Shastra are used today in the restoration and conservation of heritage buildings and temples. Conservationists follow the guidelines laid down in Shilpa Shastra to ensure that the structures retain their original aesthetic and spiritual integrity.

Many architects and urban planners are revisiting Shilpa Shastra for its ecological and sustainable principles. The alignment of buildings with natural elements such as wind and sunlight, as recommended by Shilpa Shastra, is seen as a means to create sustainable and energy-efficient designs in modern urban settings. There is also a renewed interest in the traditional crafts and artisanal techniques described in Shilpa Shastra. Government initiatives and non-governmental organizations are working to preserve these crafts, ensuring that the skills of traditional artisans are passed down to future generations.

Challenges and Preservation Efforts

Many temples, palaces, and historic monuments built according to Shilpa Shastra principles are now at risk due to neglect, environmental damage, or inappropriate restoration efforts. Conservation of these heritage structures often involves modern materials and techniques that are incompatible with the original Shilpa Shastra guidelines, leading to loss of architectural integrity. Despite these challenges, various efforts are being made at individual, institutional, and governmental levels to preserve and revive Shilpa Shastra's principles in art, architecture, and craft. These initiatives aim to bridge the gap between traditional knowledge and modern needs while maintaining the cultural and spiritual essence of the ancient system.

Government and Institutional Support

The Indian government, through organizations like the Archaeological Survey of India (ASI) and Indian National Trust for Art and Cultural Heritage (INTACH), is actively involved in the preservation of monuments and heritage structures built according to Shilpa Shastra. These organizations carry out restoration projects, ensuring that traditional materials and techniques are used to maintain the authenticity of the structures. Government programs such as Hunar Haat and Skill India promote traditional craftsmanship by offering financial assistance and training programs for artisans working in crafts rooted in Shilpa Shastra. These initiatives aim to sustain the livelihood of artisans while promoting traditional arts and crafts in modern markets.

Educational Initiatives and Training Programs

Several institutions and universities across India, such as the School of Planning and Architecture (SPA) and Banaras Hindu University (BHU), offer specialized courses in traditional Indian architecture and craftsmanship, including subjects related to Shilpa Shastra. These programs aim to educate students about the philosophical and technical aspects of traditional art forms and architecture, encouraging the integration of Shilpa Shastra principles in modern design. Additionally, traditional learning centers and training workshops have been set up in regions with a strong heritage of Shilpa Shastra-based art, such as Tamil Nadu and Rajasthan. These programs teach the next generation of artisans the skills and knowledge passed down through their ancestors, ensuring the continuity of traditional practices.

Cultural Festivals and Art Exhibitions

Cultural festivals, craft fairs, and art exhibitions serve as platforms to showcase and celebrate traditional arts and crafts governed by Shilpa Shastra. Events like the Surajkund Mela, Kala Ghoda Arts Festival, and Dastkari Haat Samiti provide a venue for artisans to demonstrate their skills and sell their handmade products, thus promoting traditional craftsmanship. These festivals not only help sustain the livelihoods of artisans but also raise public awareness about the importance of preserving these ancient art forms. Such events encourage cultural exchange and attract both domestic and international attention.

Translation and Publication of Ancient Texts

Efforts are being made to translate and publish ancient texts on Shilpa Shastra, making them more accessible to contemporary scholars, architects, and artisans. Several scholars are working on producing commentaries and modern interpretations of these texts, bridging the gap between ancient practices and contemporary applications. Projects to digitize ancient manuscripts related to Shilpa Shastra are also underway, ensuring that the knowledge is preserved for future generations and made available to a global audience.

Artisan Support and Cooperative Models

Several non-governmental organizations (NGOs) and cooperatives are working to provide direct support to artisans involved in traditional crafts. These organizations offer training, marketing assistance, and financial aid to help artisans sustain their craft in a modern economy. Cooperative models, where artisans collaborate to produce and market their products collectively, have proven successful in ensuring fair wages and reducing exploitation by middlemen. This model helps artisans maintain the quality and authenticity of their work while also reaching larger markets.

Sustainable and Eco-friendly Design Movements

There is a growing movement toward sustainable architecture that draws on the principles of Shilpa Shastra, particularly its emphasis on natural materials and harmony with the environment. Architects and urban planners are revisiting the principles of Vastu Shastra (a component of Shilpa Shastra that deals with spatial arrangement and building orientation) to design energy-efficient buildings that integrate natural elements like sunlight, wind, and water. This eco-friendly approach not only aligns with modern sustainability goals but also ensures that ancient knowledge systems like Shilpa Shastra remain relevant in the contemporary world.

Heritage Tourism and Temple Restoration

Heritage tourism has become an important driver in preserving structures built according to Shilpa Shastra principles. Temples and monuments, particularly in states like Tamil Nadu, Kerala, and Rajasthan, attract millions of tourists each year. Revenue generated from heritage tourism often funds conservation and restoration efforts, ensuring that these ancient structures are maintained for future generations. Temple restoration projects, sponsored by government and private organizations, have revived interest in Shilpa Shastra. These projects involve the reconstruction or preservation of ancient temples using traditional methods, thus preserving the architectural heritage.

Conclusion

In conclusion, Shilp Shastra remains an integral part of India's cultural heritage, influencing art and architecture for centuries. Its principles and techniques are not only foundational to historical practices but also serve as a source of inspiration for contemporary artists and designers. By embracing the wisdom of Shilp Shastra, new generations are ensuring that the legacy of traditional craftsmanship endures, adapting it to the modern world while maintaining its profound cultural significance. As this rich heritage continues to evolve, it fosters a deeper appreciation for the intricate relationship between art, spirituality, and the cultural identity of India.

Questions to Improve Learning

1. What is Shilpa Shastra, and how does it contribute to Indian art and architecture?
2. What are the primary subjects covered by Shilpa Shastra?
3. How does Shilpa Shastra define the concept of Vastu in relation to sculpture and temple architecture?
4. What is the significance of proportions and measurements (Tala) in the creation of statues and structures in Shilpa Shastra?
5. How does Shilpa Shastra guide the depiction of gods and deities in sculptures?
6. What are the different types of iconography (Pratima Lakshana) described in Shilpa Shastra for creating idols?

7. What role does geometry and symmetry play in the construction of temples according to Shilpa Shastra?

8. How does Shilpa Shastra influence the design of Dravida, Nagara, and Vesara styles of temple architecture?

9. How does Shilpa Shastra address the construction of various forms of decorative art like carvings, pillars, and gateways?

10. How does Shilpa Shastra influence modern Indian architectural practices, especially in temple construction and sculpture?

CHAPTER EIGHT

Nyaya Shastra: The System of Logic and Justice in Indian Philosophy

Nyaya Shastra (Sanskrit: न्याय शास्त्र) is one of the six orthodox schools of Indian philosophy, known for its systematic study of logic, epistemology, and the principles of reasoning. Emerging around the 2nd century BCE, Nyaya Shastra serves as both a philosophical discipline and a methodology for establishing valid knowledge and just reasoning. The word "Nyaya" translates to "justice" or "rule," reflecting the tradition's emphasis on logical reasoning as a means to attain truth and justice in knowledge and moral action. At its core, Nyaya Shastra aims to provide tools for sound reasoning and critical thinking, distinguishing valid arguments from fallacies. It also examines the nature of knowledge, belief, and doubt, addressing fundamental questions about perception, inference, and testimony. Over the centuries, Nyaya has influenced various aspects of Indian thought, including philosophy, jurisprudence, and ethics, making it a significant component of the Indian intellectual heritage.

This chapter explores the origins and historical development of Nyaya Shastra, its key principles and concepts, its relevance in philosophical discourse, and its application in contemporary contexts.

Historical Background and Development of Nyaya Shastra

The roots of Nyaya Shastra can be traced back to the *Nyaya Sutras*, attributed to the sage Gautama (also known as Akshapada) in the 2nd century BCE. These sutras are foundational texts that outline the basic principles of logic, epistemology, and argumentation. The Nyaya Sutras consist of a concise and systematic presentation of arguments, definitions, and discussions, serving as a guide for practitioners of Nyaya philosophy. The development of Nyaya continued through the centuries, with significant contributions from scholars and philosophers such as Udayana, Jayanta Bhatta, and Vatsyayana. Their works expanded upon the ideas presented in the Nyaya Sutras, addressing various aspects of logic, epistemology, and the philosophy of language. Notable texts include Udayana's *Nyaya Kusumanjali* and Vatsyayana's *Nyaya Bhashya*, which provided commentaries and interpretations of the original sutras.

As a distinct school of thought, Nyaya engaged in dialogues with other philosophical traditions, including Buddhism, Jainism, and Vedanta. The interaction between these schools led to the refinement of logical methods and epistemological theories, fostering a rich intellectual environment in ancient India.

Core Concepts of Nyaya Shastra

Nyaya Shastra is built on several fundamental concepts that form the basis of its philosophical inquiry. These concepts include:

Pramana (Means of Knowledge): Nyaya identifies four primary sources of valid knowledge (*pramanas*):

- **Pratyaksha (Perception)**: Direct sensory experience, which serves as the most immediate source of knowledge. Within perception, Nyaya distinguishes between two types: external perception (knowledge obtained through the five senses) and internal perception (knowledge of mental states). The reliability of perception is a significant topic, with discussions on factors that can affect sensory experiences.

- **Anumana (Inference)**: Knowledge derived from reasoning based on evidence. Inference allows individuals to make conclusions based on observed phenomena. It plays a central role in Nyaya philosophy. It consists of a syllogistic structure where a conclusion is drawn based on premises. The Nyaya framework outlines five steps in forming an inference: **(i)Pratijna (Proposition)**: The assertion or claim being made, **(ii) Hetu (Reason)**: The reason supporting the proposition. **(iii) Udaharana (Example)**: An example illustrating the reason. **(iv) Upanaya (Application)**: The application of the example to the case at hand. **(v) Nigamana (Conclusion)**: The conclusion drawn based on the preceding steps.

- **Upamana (Comparison)**: Knowledge gained through analogy or comparison with similar instances. This source is particularly relevant in cases where direct experience is unavailable.
- **Shabda (Testimony)**: Knowledge acquired through verbal communication, especially from authoritative sources, such as scriptures or experts.

Doubt and Belief: Nyaya analyzes the nature of doubt (*samsaya*) and belief (*prayojana*), distinguishing between valid and invalid forms of reasoning. The school emphasizes that doubt must be resolved through logical analysis to arrive at justified beliefs.

Logic and Fallacies: A significant focus of Nyaya is on identifying valid arguments and recognizing logical fallacies. Nyaya categorizes fallacies into various types, such as *anvaya* (affirmative fallacy), *vyatireka* (negative fallacy), and *sapaksha* (wrong analogy), providing a comprehensive framework for evaluating arguments.

The Nyaya System of Argumentation

The Nyaya system of argumentation is characterized by its structured approach to reasoning and debate. The following components are essential for effective argumentation in Nyaya Shastra:

Syllogism (Vyapti): Nyaya emphasizes the importance of syllogism in reasoning. A valid syllogism consists of three propositions: a major premise, a minor premise, and a conclusion. The relationship between the premises must be established to ensure the validity of the argument.

Types of Arguments: Nyaya classifies arguments into two main types:

- **Direct Argument (Sankhya)**: Arguments that present evidence directly related to the proposition.
- **Indirect Argument (Pratiksha)**: Arguments that rely on negating opposing claims or presenting counterexamples to establish the truth of the proposition.

Debate and Disputation (Vada and Jalpa): Nyaya recognizes the importance of dialectical discourse. Vada refers to constructive debate aimed at uncovering truth, while Jalpa involves contentious argumentation focused on winning rather than understanding. Nyaya encourages the practice of Vada to promote genuine inquiry and knowledge.

Criteria for Validity: To establish a valid argument, Nyaya stipulates several criteria, including:

- **Clarity**: The argument must be clear and well-defined.
- **Relevance**: The premises must be relevant to the conclusion.
- **Adequacy**: The evidence presented must be sufficient to support the conclusion.

By adhering to these principles, practitioners of Nyaya Shastra can engage in rigorous analysis and produce sound arguments.

Nyaya and Epistemology

Nyaya Shastra significantly contributes to the field of epistemology, exploring the nature of knowledge, belief, and justification. The following key aspects highlight Nyaya's epistemological framework:

i. **Nature of Knowledge**: Nyaya distinguishes between knowledge (*jnana*) and mere belief (*sadhana*). Knowledge is considered justified true belief that arises from valid sources of knowledge. Nyaya emphasizes that knowledge must be reliable and free from error.

ii. **Types of Knowledge**: Nyaya categorizes knowledge into various types, such as:

- **Samprajnata (Knowledge with Content)**: Knowledge that is clear, distinct, and involves comprehension of the object.

- **Asamprajnata (Knowledge without Content)**: A more abstract form of knowledge that may not involve specific details but still holds value in understanding.

i. **Doubt and Resolution**: Nyaya acknowledges the inevitability of doubt in the pursuit of knowledge. The tradition emphasizes the need to address doubts through logical reasoning, leading to the resolution of uncertainties and the establishment of justified beliefs.

ii. **The Role of Inference**: Inference is a crucial component of Nyaya's epistemology, allowing individuals to extend their understanding beyond direct observation. Through logical reasoning, one can arrive at conclusions based on available evidence, even when direct perception is lacking.

Nyaya and Ethics

While primarily known for its contributions to logic and epistemology, Nyaya Shastra also addresses ethical concerns and moral philosophy. Key ethical concepts in

Nyaya include:

- **Dharma (Righteousness)**: Nyaya emphasizes the importance of *dharma* as a guiding principle for ethical behavior. The pursuit of righteousness is seen as essential for individual well-being and social harmony.
- **Justice and Fairness**: The concept of *Nyaya* encompasses justice, fairness, and the establishment of moral order. The tradition advocates for the application of reason and logic in matters of ethics and justice, ensuring that decisions are made based on rationality and fairness.
- **Moral Responsibility**: Nyaya recognizes the role of individuals in shaping their ethical conduct. The tradition emphasizes that actions have consequences, and individuals must take responsibility for their choices, which aligns with the concept of karma in Indian philosophy.
- **Ethical Dilemmas**: Nyaya provides a framework for resolving ethical dilemmas through rational analysis and logical reasoning. The emphasis on clear argumentation allows practitioners to navigate complex moral situations with clarity and insight.

Nyaya and Other Indian Philosophical Schools

Nyaya Shastra's interactions with other Indian philosophical traditions have contributed to the richness of Indian thought. Notable engagements include:

- **Buddhism**: Nyaya engaged in philosophical debates with Buddhist schools, particularly concerning epistemology and the nature of reality. The Nyaya emphasis on logical reasoning provided a counterpoint to certain Buddhist views, leading to fruitful exchanges.
- **Jainism**: The Jain tradition shares certain similarities with Nyaya, particularly in its emphasis on epistemology and non-violence. Both schools explore the nature of knowledge, but their methodologies and conclusions may differ.
- **Vedanta**: Nyaya and Vedanta often intersect, particularly in discussions of metaphysics and epistemology. While Nyaya focuses on logic and reasoning, Vedanta emphasizes spiritual realization. The two schools engage in dialogues that enrich both traditions.

Nyaya's Influence on Indian Jurisprudence

Nyaya Shastra has had a profound impact on Indian jurisprudence and the legal system. Key contributions include:

- **Principles of Justice**: Nyaya emphasizes the importance of justice, fairness, and reason in legal proceedings. The principles established in Nyaya have influenced the formulation of legal norms and practices.
- **Legal Reasoning**: The emphasis on logical argumentation in Nyaya provides a foundation for legal reasoning. Legal practitioners can draw upon the Nyaya system to construct and evaluate arguments in the context of law.

- **Role of Evidence**: Nyaya's analysis of perception, inference, and testimony has shaped the understanding of evidence in legal contexts. The tradition underscores the importance of reliable evidence in establishing truth and justice.
- **Conflict Resolution**: Nyaya promotes the idea of dialogue and rational discourse in resolving disputes. This approach aligns with traditional practices of mediation and arbitration in Indian society.

Contemporary Relevance of Nyaya Shastra

In modern times, Nyaya Shastra remains relevant in various fields, including philosophy, education, and law. Key areas of contemporary significance include:

- **Critical Thinking**: The emphasis on logical reasoning and argumentation in Nyaya promotes critical thinking skills, which are essential in education and decision-making. Nyaya's principles can be applied to enhance analytical abilities in students and professionals.
- **Philosophical Inquiry**: Nyaya's exploration of epistemology and ethics continues to inspire philosophical inquiry. Modern philosophers draw upon Nyaya's insights to address contemporary issues related to knowledge, belief, and morality.
- **Legal Education**: The principles of Nyaya are integrated into legal education, emphasizing the importance of logical reasoning and argumentation in legal practice. Law students benefit from studying Nyaya as a foundational framework for understanding justice.

- **Interdisciplinary Dialogue**: Nyaya's interactions with other philosophical traditions foster interdisciplinary dialogue, encouraging collaborations between philosophy, cognitive science, psychology, and other fields.

Conclusion

Nyaya Shastra is a profound and comprehensive system of thought that emphasizes the importance of logic, reasoning, and justice in the pursuit of knowledge. With its historical roots in ancient India, Nyaya has contributed significantly to the fields of epistemology, ethics, and jurisprudence. Its structured approach to argumentation, emphasis on valid sources of knowledge, and commitment to justice have made it a cornerstone of Indian philosophy. In contemporary contexts, Nyaya Shastra remains relevant as a framework for critical thinking, legal reasoning, and ethical inquiry. By continuing to explore the principles of Nyaya, individuals and scholars can deepen their understanding of knowledge, justice, and the complexities of human existence. The enduring legacy of Nyaya Shastra is a testament to its profound impact on Indian thought and its potential to inspire future generations in their quest for truth and justice.

Practice Questions

1. What is Nyaya Shastra, and what role does it play in Indian philosophy?
2. What are the four main sources of Pramanas recognized in Nyaya Shastra?

3. How does Nyaya Shastra define the process of inference Anumana)?

4. What is the concept of Pratyaksha (perception) in Nyaya Shastra, and how is it classified?

5. How does Nyaya Shastra differentiate between valid (Prama) and invalid (Aprama) knowledge?

6. What is the role of Upamana (comparison) as a source of knowledge in Nyaya Shastra?

7. How does Nyaya Shastra define verbal testimony (Shabda) as a means of knowledge?

8. How does Nyaya Shastra address the nature and definition of Doubt (Samsaya)?

9. How does Nyaya Shastra contribute to the development of the art of debate (*Vada*) and logical argumentation?

10. How does Nyaya Shastra define Liberation (Moksha), and what role does knowledge play in achieving it?

Contribution of IKS to the World

The Indian Knowledge System (IKS) encompasses a vast array of ancient wisdom, philosophies, sciences, arts, and cultural practices that have evolved over thousands of years. With its roots in diverse fields such as philosophy, mathematics, astronomy, medicine, linguistics, and the arts, IKS has significantly influenced global knowledge traditions and continues to hold relevance in contemporary society. This chapter explores the multifaceted contributions of IKS to the world, highlighting its impact on various domains.

Mathematics and Astronomy in the Indian Knowledge System

Mathematics and astronomy have been integral components of the Indian Knowledge System (IKS), demonstrating the advanced intellectual traditions of ancient India. Indian mathematicians and astronomers made significant contributions to both fields, influencing not only their contemporaries but also shaping the development of mathematics and astronomy across the globe. This chapter explores the key developments, concepts, and figures in Indian mathematics and astronomy, highlighting their contributions and legacy.

Ancient Indian Mathematics

The foundations of Indian mathematics can be traced back to the Vedic period (c. 1500–500 BCE), where mathematical concepts were primarily applied to rituals and astronomy. The subsequent developments in mathematics led to groundbreaking discoveries and innovations.

Vedic Mathematics

- **Sutras**: The Vedas contain mathematical sutras (verses) that provide insights into various calculations, including arithmetic and geometry. These sutras emphasize techniques for efficient problem-solving and mental calculations.
- **Geometry**: The Sulba Sutras, texts associated with the Vedas, contain rules for constructing altars and sacrifices. These texts showcase an understanding of geometric principles, such as the Pythagorean Theorem, long before it was known in the West.

The Concept of Zero and the Decimal System

- **Zero**: The introduction of the concept of zero (shunya) is one of the most significant contributions of Indian mathematics. It allowed for a place-value system, facilitating calculations and the representation of large numbers.
- **Decimal System**: The decimal system, which uses base ten, was fully developed in India by the 6th century CE. Mathematicians like Aryabhata and Brahmagupta played

pivotal roles in refining this system, which became the foundation of modern arithmetic.

Notable Mathematicians

- **Aryabhata (476–550 CE)**: Aryabhata's work, *Aryabhatiya*, presents a comprehensive system of mathematics and astronomy. He introduced algebraic concepts, trigonometric functions, and the approximation of π (pi) as 3.1416.
- **Brahmagupta (598–668 CE)**: Brahmagupta's *Brahmasphutasiddhanta* addressed arithmetic operations, including rules for zero and negative numbers. He also contributed to solving quadratic equations and presented methods for finding the area of cyclic quadrilaterals.

Advanced Mathematics

- **Algebra**: Indian mathematicians made significant advancements in algebra, including the development of methods for solving linear and quadratic equations. The concept of permutations and combinations also emerged during this period.
- **Trigonometry**: Indian scholars introduced trigonometric functions and relationships, such as sine and cosine, significantly contributing to the field of astronomy.

Ancient Indian Astronomy

Indian astronomy has a rich history that is closely intertwined with mathematics. Ancient Indian astronomers made significant strides in understanding celestial bodies and their movements, influencing global astronomical thought.

Early Astronomy

- **Vedic Astronomy**: The Vedic texts include astronomical observations related to the calendar and rituals. The positioning of celestial bodies was essential for conducting accurate religious ceremonies.
- **Astronomical Instruments**: Ancient Indian astronomers developed various instruments, including the gnomon (a vertical stick used to measure shadows) and the astrolabe (a device for solving problems related to time and the position of stars).

Siddhantic Astronomy

The *Siddhantas* are classical astronomical texts that systematize astronomical knowledge. Key texts include:

- **Aryabhata's Aryabhatiya**: Aryabhata proposed a heliocentric model of the solar system and calculated the length of the solar year as approximately 365.358 days. He also introduced methods for calculating planetary positions.
- **Surya Siddhanta**: This text, dating back to around the 4th century CE, provides mathematical calculations related to astronomy. It discusses the movements of celestial bodies, eclipses, and the calculation of time.

Notable Astronomers

- **Varahamihira (505–587 CE)**: A prominent astronomer and mathematician, Varahamihira's work, *Pancha Siddhantika*, discusses various astronomical systems and observations. He contributed to understanding planetary positions and eclipses.
- **Brahmagupta**: In addition to his mathematical contributions, Brahmagupta's works in astronomy laid the foundation for calculating lunar and solar eclipses and understanding planetary motions.

Influence on Global Mathematics and Astronomy

The contributions of Indian mathematicians and astronomers had a lasting impact on both fields worldwide, influencing subsequent developments in various cultures:

Transmission of Knowledge

- The concepts of zero and the decimal system were transmitted to the Islamic world through translations of Indian texts, influencing medieval European mathematics. The introduction of Arabic numerals is a direct result of this transmission.
- Indian astronomical works reached the Islamic scholars, who built upon this knowledge, leading to significant advancements during the Islamic Golden Age.

Influence on European Mathematics

- The adoption of Indian numeral systems in Europe during the Renaissance facilitated advancements in mathematics and science. Mathematicians like

Fibonacci acknowledged the significance of Indian mathematics in his work, *Liber Abaci.*

- The mathematical techniques developed in India, including the rules of algebra and arithmetic, provided the groundwork for modern mathematics.

Contemporary Relevance

The contributions of IKS to mathematics and astronomy continue to hold relevance in contemporary times:

Education and Curriculum

- The principles of Indian mathematics are increasingly recognized in educational curricula, emphasizing the importance of critical thinking and problem-solving.
- Ancient texts and mathematical sutras are studied for their pedagogical value and their application in modern teaching methods.

Space Research and Technology

- Indian advancements in astronomy have inspired contemporary research in space science and technology. The Indian Space Research Organisation (ISRO) continues to build on this legacy, contributing to global space exploration efforts.

Interdisciplinary Research

- The interplay between mathematics, astronomy, and other scientific disciplines fosters interdisciplinary research, encouraging collaboration between fields such as physics, engineering, and computer science.

Mathematics and astronomy in the Indian Knowledge System exemplify the profound intellectual achievements of ancient India. The innovations in mathematical concepts, such as zero and the decimal system, along with significant contributions to astronomy, have left an indelible mark on global knowledge traditions. The legacy of Indian mathematicians and astronomers continues to inspire contemporary scholarship, promoting an understanding of the interconnectedness of human knowledge and the pursuit of truth in both fields. As we explore the cosmos and unravel the mysteries of mathematics, the wisdom of IKS serves as a guiding light, reminding us of the rich heritage that shapes our understanding of the universe.

Role of Physics in the Indian Knowledge System

Ancient Concepts of Physics

- **Philosophical Foundations**: Ancient Indian texts like the *Sankhya* and *Yoga Sutras* explore fundamental concepts of nature and the universe, emphasizing the relationship between matter, energy, and consciousness. These philosophical inquiries laid the groundwork for understanding physical phenomena.
- **Space and Time**: The Indian cosmological model, as presented in texts like the *Vishnu Purana*, describes the universe's structure, dimensions, and cycles of creation and dissolution, reflecting an understanding of space and time that aligns with modern cosmology.

Mechanics and Motion

- **Archaeological Evidence**: Evidence of early mechanical devices, such as water clocks and simple machines, showcases the practical application of physics in ancient Indian technology.
- **Bhaskaracharya's Contributions**: The mathematician and astronomer Bhaskara II, in his work *Siddhanta Shiromani*, discussed concepts of motion and mechanics, including the laws of falling bodies and planetary motion, which have influenced later scientific thought.

Innovations in Astronomy

- **Astronomical Instruments**: Ancient Indian astronomers developed sophisticated instruments like the gnomon and the astrolabe, contributing to celestial navigation and timekeeping.
- **Calendar Systems**: Indian astronomers created accurate calendars based on the lunar and solar cycles, facilitating agricultural practices and rituals.

Role of Chemistry in the Indian Knowledge System

Alchemy and Early Chemistry

- **Rasa Shastra**: The ancient Indian practice of alchemy, known as *Rasa Shastra*, focused on the transmutation of materials, particularly metals, and the creation of herbal compounds. Texts like *Rasa Ratna Samuccaya* elaborate on the medicinal properties of various substances.

- **Herbal Preparations**: Early chemists in India developed methods for extracting and refining medicinal compounds from plants, contributing to traditional medicine and pharmacology.

Ayurvedic Chemistry

- **Herbal Formulations**: Ayurveda incorporates principles of chemistry in the preparation of herbal medicines, emphasizing the importance of chemical properties and interactions in healing practices.
- **Medicinal Processes**: The *Sushruta Samhita* describes processes such as distillation and calcination, which are foundational to modern chemistry, demonstrating a sophisticated understanding of chemical transformations.

Metallurgy

- **Ancient Metallurgical Practices**: India has a rich history of metallurgy, with significant contributions to the extraction and processing of metals such as iron and zinc. The production of high-quality steel, known as Wootz steel, highlights advanced metallurgical techniques.
- **Artistry and Chemistry**: The use of chemical knowledge in metalworking, pottery, and dyeing techniques contributed to the development of various crafts and artistic traditions in India.

Role of Botany in the Indian Knowledge System

Traditional Knowledge of Plants

- **Ethnobotany**: Ancient Indian texts document extensive knowledge of plants and their uses, including medicinal, culinary, and spiritual applications. The *Rigveda* and *Atharvaveda* reference various plants for their therapeutic properties.
- **Medicinal Plants**: Ayurveda extensively employs herbal remedies derived from local flora, providing insights into the medicinal properties of plants and their applications in health care.

Agriculture and Crop Cultivation

- **Sustainable Agricultural Practices**: Ancient Indian agriculture emphasized sustainable practices, including crop rotation, intercropping, and organic farming. This understanding of botany contributed to food security and environmental sustainability.
- **Varietal Development**: Traditional Indian farmers selectively bred plants to enhance yield and resilience, laying the foundation for modern agricultural practices.

Conservation and Biodiversity

- **Sacred Groves**: Cultural practices in India, such as the preservation of sacred groves, reflect an early understanding of biodiversity conservation and ecological balance.

- **Botanical Gardens and Herbal Gardens**: The establishment of botanical gardens and herbal gardens in ancient India contributed to the preservation of plant species and the study of their ecological and medicinal significance.

The Indian Knowledge System encompasses a rich tapestry of knowledge across various scientific disciplines, including physics, chemistry, and botany. These fields have contributed to a holistic understanding of the natural world, emphasizing the interconnectedness of all life forms and the importance of sustainable practices. The legacy of IKS continues to influence modern science, culture, and practices, highlighting the value of traditional knowledge in addressing contemporary challenges. As we move forward, recognizing and integrating these ancient insights can contribute to a more sustainable and equitable future.

Metal Technology and Mining Techniques in Ancient India

Ancient India was renowned for its advanced metal technology, which played a crucial role in various domains such as agriculture, warfare, craftsmanship, and trade. The understanding of mining, smelting, and metallurgy laid the foundation for producing high-quality metals and tools. This document explores the types of metals used, mining techniques, and tools and techniques for metal smelting in ancient India.

Types of Metals in Ancient India

Ancient India utilized a variety of metals, each serving different purposes:

Copper

- **Usage**: Copper was one of the first metals used by humans and was primarily used for making tools, ornaments, and utensils.
- **Historical Significance**: The Indus Valley Civilization (c. 3300–1300 BCE) produced copper artifacts, showcasing advanced metallurgy and craftsmanship.

Bronze

- **Alloy Composition**: Bronze is an alloy of copper and tin, known for its durability and resistance to corrosion.
- **Applications**: Bronze was used for weapons, tools, and sculptures, with notable examples like the bronze figurines of the Indus Valley and the famous bronze statues of deities.

Iron

- **Iron Age**: The Iron Age in India (c. 1200 BCE) marked significant advancements in technology. Iron was preferred for its strength and versatility.
- **Wootz Steel**: Ancient Indians developed Wootz steel, a high-quality steel known for its sharpness and resilience, which was highly sought after globally.

Gold and Silver

- **Precious Metals**: Gold and silver were primarily used for jewellery, ornaments, and currency. The craftsmanship of goldsmiths and silversmiths was highly developed.
- **Cultural Importance**: Gold and silver held significant cultural and religious value, often used in rituals and as

offerings.

Mining Techniques in Ancient India

Mining was a vital industry in ancient India, facilitating the extraction of various metals. Techniques used included:

Open-Pit Mining

- **Method**: This technique involved removing surface layers of soil and rock to access ore deposits. It was suitable for extracting copper, iron, and other metals.
- **Example**: The open-pit mining of copper ores in places like Khetri in Rajasthan is well-documented.

Underground Mining

- **Method**: For deeper deposits, underground mining techniques were employed, which included shaft mining and horizontal tunneling.
- **Example**: The mining of gold and silver in the Kolar Gold Fields utilized extensive underground mining methods.

Surface Mining

- **Method**: Surface mining techniques such as quarrying were used for obtaining stones and some metal ores.
- **Example**: The extraction of iron ore from the mines in the Singhbhum region followed surface mining techniques.

Tools and Techniques for Metal Smelting

Metal smelting involved various techniques and tools that enabled the transformation of raw ores into usable metals. Key aspects include:

Furnaces

Ancient India utilized different types of furnaces for smelting metals, including:

- **Pit Furnaces**: Simple pits lined with clay were used for smelting smaller quantities of metal.
- **Blast Furnaces**: More advanced furnaces, often made from clay or brick, were used for large-scale metal production, especially iron.
- The *bloomery furnace*, which produced wrought iron, was a common type of furnace used during the Iron Age in India.

Smelting Techniques

- **Direct Reduction**: This method involved heating the ore in the presence of carbon (usually charcoal) to reduce it to metal. This technique was primarily used for copper and iron.
- **Reverberatory Furnace**: A more advanced technique that allowed for better temperature control and efficiency in smelting metals. It facilitated the production of higher-quality metals.

Tools Used in Metalworking

- **Hammers and Anvils**: Essential tools for shaping and forging metals. Blacksmiths used hammers of various sizes for different tasks.

- **Tongs**: Used to handle hot metals during forging and shaping.
- **Chisels and Saws**: Employed for intricate work, including engraving and cutting metal.
- **Molds and Casting Techniques**: Molding techniques were used for casting bronze and other alloys into desired shapes.

Examples of Metal Technology in Ancient India

Copper Technology

- **Artifacts**: Numerous copper artifacts, including tools, utensils, and ornaments, have been discovered from the Indus Valley Civilization.
- **Techniques**: The lost-wax casting method was utilized for producing intricate copper figurines.

Bronze Sculpture

- **Dancing Girl of Mohenjo-Daro**: This famous bronze statue exemplifies advanced casting techniques and artistic skills of the period.
- **Bronze Weapons**: Weapons such as swords and shields were crafted from bronze, demonstrating the utility and craftsmanship involved.

Iron Technology

- **Iron Pillar of Delhi**: An example of advanced metallurgy, this iron pillar (c. 400 CE) is known for its rust-resistant properties, showcasing the skill in producing high-quality wrought iron.
- **Wootz Steel**: The development of Wootz steel allowed for the production of superior blades, which became famous worldwide.

Ancient India's metal technology, mining techniques, and expertise in smelting were critical to the civilization's advancement and cultural richness. The understanding of various metals, innovative mining methods, and sophisticated smelting techniques contributed to India's historical significance in metallurgy. The legacy of these practices continues to influence modern metallurgy and technology, reflecting the profound knowledge embedded in the Indian Knowledge System.

Town Planning and Temple Architecture in Ancient India

Ancient India was characterized by advanced urban planning and architectural brilliance, especially evident in its towns and temples. This document explores the principles of town planning and the features of temple architecture, highlighting their historical significance and cultural impact. Ancient Indian towns were designed with meticulous planning, reflecting an understanding of urban needs, social organization, and environmental considerations. Major urban centers like those of the Indus Valley Civilization and later historical cities exemplify advanced planning techniques.

Indus Valley Civilization (3300–1300 BCE)

- **Grid Layout**: Cities like Mohenjo-Daro and Harappa featured a grid-like layout, with streets laid out at right angles, ensuring systematic organization. Roads were wide and well-planned, facilitating movement and trade.
- **Drainage Systems**: One of the remarkable features of Indus Valley cities was their sophisticated drainage system. Well-built drains and sanitation systems were laid out beneath the streets, showcasing advanced engineering and public health awareness.
- **Residential Areas**: Houses were built using standardized bricks and often had multiple stories, with wells and bathrooms, indicating a focus on hygiene and comfort. The residential sectors were separated from commercial and industrial zones, reflecting a planned approach to urban living.

Later Historical Towns

- **Nagar and Purana**: The terms *nagar* (town) and *purana* (fortified town) denote different types of settlements. While nagars were generally open and organized, puranas had fortified walls for protection.
- **Palaces and Administrative Centers**: Towns developed during the Maurya, Gupta, and medieval periods featured palaces, administrative offices, and markets, emphasizing political and economic organization.
- **Water Management**: Ancient towns often included tanks, reservoirs, and wells for water supply. The management of water resources was critical for agriculture and urban life.

Influence of Religion on Town Planning

- **Sacred Geometry**: The layout of towns often reflected sacred geometry, aligning with cosmic principles. Temples were typically situated at the town center, indicating the importance of religion in social life.
- **Cultural Centers**: Many ancient towns became cultural and religious centers, attracting pilgrims and scholars, further enhancing their significance.

Ayurveda

Ayurveda, an ancient system of medicine that originated in India more than 5,000 years ago, is often referred to as the "science of life" (from the Sanskrit words "Ayus," meaning life, and "Veda," meaning knowledge). This holistic approach to health and wellness integrates physical, mental, and spiritual well-being, emphasizing the importance of balance in all aspects of life. This document provides an in-depth introduction to Ayurveda, exploring its history, foundational principles, diagnostic techniques, treatment modalities, and contemporary relevance. Ayurveda has its roots in the Vedic texts, which are the oldest scriptures of Hindu philosophy. The foundational texts of Ayurveda, including the *Charaka Samhita*, *Sushruta Samhita*, and *Ashtanga Hridaya*, were written between 600 BCE and 200 CE. These texts compiled knowledge from various sources, including oral traditions, observations, and practices that had been passed down through generations.

The Five Elements (Pancha Mahabhuta) Ayurveda posits that the universe, including the human body, is made up of five fundamental elements:

- **Earth (Prithvi)**: Represents stability and structure.

- **Water (Apas)**: Symbolizes fluidity and cohesion.
- **Fire (Tejas)**: Embodies transformation and metabolism.
- **Air (Vayu)**: Represents movement and communication.
- **Space (Akasha)**: Denotes the expansiveness and connectivity of all things.

These elements combine to form three doshas (biological energies) in the body.

Doshas

The three doshas—Vata, Pitta, and Kapha—are the key concepts in Ayurveda, representing different combinations of the five elements:

- **Vata**: Comprised of air and space, Vata governs movement, circulation, and communication. It is responsible for bodily functions such as breathing and muscle contraction.
- **Pitta**: Made up of fire and water, Pitta controls digestion, metabolism, and energy production. It is associated with the body's transformative processes.
- **Kapha**: Formed from earth and water, Kapha provides structure, stability, and lubrication. It plays a crucial role in maintaining body weight and immune function.

Each individual possesses a unique constitution (Prakriti) determined by the dominant dosha(s), which influences their physical, emotional, and mental characteristics.

The Concept of Balance

A central tenet of Ayurveda is the belief that health is a state of balance among the doshas, as well as between the mind, body, and spirit. Disharmony or imbalance in any of these areas can lead to disease. Therefore, Ayurveda emphasizes preventative measures and lifestyle modifications to maintain harmony.

Diagnosis in Ayurveda

Ayurvedic diagnosis relies on comprehensive assessment techniques that focus on understanding the individual as a whole. The primary methods include:

- **Prakriti Assessment:** Determining an individual's unique constitution (Prakriti) is essential for personalized treatment. This assessment includes evaluating the dominant dosha(s) and understanding their characteristics.
- **Samprapti (Pathogenesis):** Samprapti refers to the process of understanding the root cause of a disease. It involves examining the disease's origin, progression, and manifestations in the body.

Diagnostic Techniques

Ayurveda employs various diagnostic methods, including:

- **Darshan (Observation):** Visual assessment of the patient, including complexion, posture, and movement.
- **Sparshan (Touch):** Palpation to assess pulse, temperature, and texture of tissues.

- **Prashna (Questioning)**: Comprehensive inquiry into the patient's history, lifestyle, dietary habits, and emotional state.
- **Nadi Pariksha (Pulse Diagnosis)**: A specialized technique that analyzes the pulse's qualities to determine the balance of doshas and the state of health.

Treatment Modalities in Ayurveda

Ayurvedic treatments aim to restore balance and promote holistic well-being through a variety of approaches:

Diet and Nutrition (Ahara): Diet plays a critical role in Ayurveda, with food being viewed as medicine. Ayurvedic practitioners recommend personalized dietary plans based on individual Prakriti and current imbalances. Key concepts include:

- **Sattvic Foods:** Foods that promote purity and health, such as fresh fruits, vegetables, and whole grains.
- **Rajasic Foods:** Stimulating foods that may lead to agitation or hyperactivity, such as spicy or overly processed foods.
- **Tamasic Foods:** Heavy or stale foods that can contribute to lethargy and imbalance, like processed and canned items.

Herbal Remedies: Ayurveda employs a vast array of herbs and natural substances for therapeutic purposes. Common herbs include:

- **Turmeric (Curcuma longa)**: Known for its anti-inflammatory properties and ability to enhance digestion.

- **Ashwagandha (Withania somnifera):** An adaptogen that helps the body cope with stress and boosts vitality.
- **Ginger (Zingiber officinale):** Used for its digestive and anti-inflammatory effects.

Panchakarma: Panchakarma is a detoxification and rejuvenation therapy designed to cleanse the body of toxins (ama) and restore balance. It includes five primary procedures:

- Vamana: Therapeutic vomiting to expel excess Kapha.
- Virechana: Purgation therapy to eliminate excess Pitta.
- Basti: Enema therapy using herbal oils and decoctions to balance Vata.
- Nasyam: Nasal administration of herbal formulations for respiratory health.
- Raktamokshana: Bloodletting techniques for purifying the blood.

Lifestyle Modifications (Vihara)

Ayurveda emphasizes the importance of a balanced lifestyle to maintain health. Recommendations may include:

- Regular Exercise: Tailored to individual dosha and capabilities.
- Meditation and Yoga: Practices that promote mental clarity and emotional balance.
- Daily Routines (Dinacharya): Establishing daily rituals for eating, sleeping, and self-care.

Influence of Ayurveda

Ayurveda has significantly influenced not only Indian culture but also various systems of medicine across the world, including Traditional Chinese Medicine (TCM) and Unani medicine. Its principles of holistic health and natural healing resonate with modern wellness practices, leading to its growing popularity in the global health landscape.

- **Global Acceptance:** In recent decades, Ayurveda has gained international recognition as a holistic approach to health and wellness. Many people are turning to Ayurvedic practices for preventive care, stress management, and chronic disease management.
- **Integration with Modern Medicine:** There is an increasing trend to integrate Ayurvedic principles with conventional medicine. This approach emphasizes a holistic understanding of health, considering lifestyle factors and preventive measures alongside pharmacological interventions.
- **Research and Development:** Ongoing research in pharmacognosy and clinical studies continues to validate Ayurvedic herbs and treatments. This scientific exploration seeks to bridge traditional knowledge with modern methodologies, ensuring the safety and efficacy of Ayurvedic practices.

Ayurveda represents a profound and timeless system of medicine that offers valuable insights into health, wellness, and the interconnectedness of mind, body, and spirit. Its holistic approach emphasizes prevention, personalized care, and the importance of maintaining balance in all aspects of life. As Ayurveda gains prominence in the global health arena, it continues to inspire individuals to seek a deeper understanding of their health and well-being, fostering a more integrated approach to healthcare. Embracing Ayurvedic principles can lead to a healthier, more balanced life, rooted in ancient wisdom and adapted for modern needs.

Art and Traditions in Indian Culture

India, with its rich tapestry of history, culture, and spirituality, boasts an extensive array of art forms and traditions that reflect the diversity and depth of its civilization. This document delves into the history and origin of Indian art and traditions, explores the concept of *64 Kala* (the 64 arts), and examines the science behind various traditions and rituals.

Ancient Roots

Indian art can be traced back to prehistoric times, with evidence of artistic expression found in rock paintings in regions like Bhimbetka and the caves of Ajanta and Ellora. These early artworks often depicted scenes of daily life, animals, and spiritual beliefs, serving both aesthetic and communicative purposes.

Religious Influences

Religion has played a pivotal role in shaping Indian art and traditions. Hinduism, Buddhism, and Jainism have significantly influenced artistic expressions, from temple architecture to sculpture and painting. The Maurya and Gupta periods marked a golden age of art, where monumental sculptures, intricate carvings, and frescoes flourished.

- **Hindu Art**: Temple architecture, with its intricate carvings of deities and mythological narratives, reflects the spiritual beliefs and cultural values of the time. The Khajuraho temples and Brihadeeswarar Temple exemplify this rich tradition.
- **Buddhist Art**: Stupas and monastic complexes, such as those found in Sanchi and Nalanda, illustrate the Buddhist principles of simplicity and meditation. The sculptures in the Ajanta caves depict the life of the Buddha and Jataka tales.
- **Jain Art**: Known for its meticulous detail and emphasis on non-violence, Jain art features exquisite marble sculptures and temple architecture, such as the Dilwara Temples in Rajasthan.

Regional Variations

India's vast geography and cultural diversity have led to the evolution of distinct regional art forms. Each region boasts its unique styles, techniques, and themes:

- **Madhubani**: Originating from Bihar, this folk art form employs vibrant colors and intricate patterns, often depicting mythological themes and nature.
- **Warli**: A tribal art form from Maharashtra, Warli art uses simple geometric shapes to portray daily life, rituals, and nature, emphasizing harmony with the environment.
- **Tanjore Painting**: Hailing from Tamil Nadu, Tanjore paintings are characterized by their rich colors, intricate details, and the use of gold foil, often depicting Hindu deities.

Skill Enhancement with 64 Kala

The concept of *64 Kala* is a significant aspect of Indian culture, referring to the comprehensive set of arts and crafts that encompass a wide array of skills. These arts are traditionally believed to be essential for personal development, social harmony, and aesthetic appreciation. The term *Kala* translates to "art" or "skill," and the *64 Kala* are classified into various categories, including performing arts, fine arts, craftsmanship, and practical skills. They embody the essence of creativity and expertise, emphasizing the importance of mastering diverse talents for holistic growth.

Categories of 64 Kala

While there are different interpretations of the *64 Kala*, they are generally grouped into the following categories:

i. **Performing Arts**: This includes dance forms (Bharatanatyam, Kathak), music (vocal and instrumental), and theater (Natya).

ii. **Fine Arts**: Painting, sculpture, and architecture fall under this category, encompassing various styles and techniques.

iii. **Craftsmanship**: Skills such as pottery, weaving, metalwork, and jewelry making highlight the artisanal traditions of India.

iv. **Culinary Arts**: Cooking and food presentation reflect regional flavors and traditions, showcasing the significance of gastronomy in culture.

v. **Practical Skills**: Skills like agriculture, gardening, and medicinal practices emphasize the connection between humans and nature.

Learning and Transmission

Traditionally, the *64 Kala* were taught through *Guru-Shishya Parampara*, the master-disciple system, where knowledge was imparted through hands-on experience and oral traditions. This system fostered a deep connection between the teacher and student, ensuring the preservation and evolution of these skills.

Contemporary Relevance

In modern times, the *64 Kala* serves as a framework for skill development and cultural education. Various organizations and institutions promote these arts through workshops, courses, and exhibitions, fostering creativity and preserving cultural heritage.

Science behind Our Traditions and Rituals

Indian traditions and rituals are deeply rooted in spiritual beliefs, but they also encompass scientific principles that promote well-being, harmony, and sustainability.

Rituals and Their Significance: Rituals in India are performed to mark important life events, religious observances, and seasonal changes. These rituals often hold symbolic meaning and serve various purposes, including:

- **Connection with the Divine**: Rituals such as *puja* (worship) are performed to honor deities and seek blessings. The use of specific materials (flowers, incense, food) in these rituals is believed to attract positive energies.

- **Community Cohesion**: Festivals and communal rituals foster social bonds and reinforce cultural identity. Events like Diwali, Holi, and Eid involve collective participation, enhancing social harmony.

Scientific Underpinnings: Many traditional practices have been validated by modern science, revealing their practical benefits:

- **Ayurveda and Natural Healing**: Ayurvedic practices, including herbal remedies, dietary guidelines, and detoxification techniques, are grounded in principles of balance and harmony. Research supports the efficacy of various Ayurvedic treatments for promoting health and preventing disease.
- **Astrology and Timing**: The timing of rituals and ceremonies is often determined by astrological calculations. This practice emphasizes aligning human activities with natural cycles, such as lunar phases, which can impact agriculture and well-being.
- **Sustainable Practices**: Traditional agricultural practices, such as crop rotation and organic farming, promote soil health and biodiversity. These methods are increasingly recognized for their sustainability and ecological benefits.

The Psychological Aspect: Rituals and traditions often provide psychological comfort and a sense of belonging. Engaging in familiar practices during significant life events can reduce stress and foster emotional well-being. The act of participation in communal rituals creates a shared experience, reinforcing community ties.

Conclusion

The contributions of Indian Knowledge Systems to the world are vast and diverse, reflecting India's rich cultural and intellectual heritage. One of the most significant contributions is in mathematics, where IKS introduced concepts such as zero, the decimal system, and advanced algebra, fundamentally influencing global mathematics. In astronomy, ancient Indian astronomers developed sophisticated calculations and models, including early heliocentric theories. The realm of medicine has also been enriched by traditional systems like Ayurveda and Siddha, which offer holistic approaches to health emphasizing prevention and natural remedies. Philosophically, Indian schools of thought, including Vedanta and Buddhism, have profoundly impacted global discussions on ethics, existence, and consciousness. The practice of yoga, which promotes physical, mental, and spiritual well-being, has gained worldwide recognition and adoption. Together, these contributions highlight the profound and enduring impact of Indian Knowledge Systems on various fields and cultures across the globe.

CHAPTER TEN

References

The Indian Knowledge System (IKS) is a vast and ancient body of knowledge encompassing a variety of disciplines, philosophies, sciences, and practices that originated in India. These systems have evolved over millennia and continue to influence various fields today, from mathematics and medicine to philosophy, linguistics, and architecture. Below are key references to different branches of the Indian Knowledge System:

Here is a list of references and recommended readings to explore the Indian Knowledge System (IKS), covering various disciplines such as philosophy, science, mathematics, medicine, architecture, and more:

1. "Indian Knowledge Systems" by Kapil Kapoor
2. "The Spirit of Indian Culture" by Sisir Kumar Mitra
3. "Foundations of Indian Culture" by Sri Aurobindo
4. "India's Knowledge Systems" edited by Subhash Kak, T. R. N. Rao, and K. S. Valdiya
5. "Indian Knowledge Systems (Volume I & II)" by Mahesh C. Raturi
6. "The Upanishads" translated by Eknath Easwaran
7. "Indian Philosophy" by Sarvepalli Radhakrishnan
8. "The Essentials of Indian Philosophy" by M. Hiriyanna

9. "The History of Indian Mathematics" by C. N. Srinivasiengar

10. "Geometry in Ancient and Medieval India" by T. A. Sarasvati Amma

11. "Aryabhatiya of Aryabhata" translated by K. S. Shukla and K. V. Sarma

12. "A Concise History of Science in India" edited by D. M. Bose, S. N. Sen, and B. V. Subbarayappa

13. "Charaka Samhita" translated by R. K. Sharma and Bhagwan Dash

14. "Sushruta Samhita" translated by Kaviraj Kunja Lal Bhishagratna

15. "Ayurveda: The Science of Self-Healing" by Dr. Vasant Lad

16. "The Ashtadhyayi of Panini" translated by Srisa Chandra Vasu

17. "The Vakyapadiya of Bhartrhari" translated by K. A. Subramania Iyer

18. "Sanskrit Non-Translatables: The Importance of Sanskritizing English" by Rajiv Malhotra and Satyanarayana Dasa Babaji

19. "Natya Shastra" by Bharata Muni, translated by Manomohan Ghosh

20. "The Rasa Theory" by Kapila Vatsyayan

21. "Vastu Shastra: The Ancient Indian Science of Architecture" by B. B. Puri

22. "Silpa-Sastra" by Alice Boner

23. "Arthashastra" by Kautilya (Chanakya), translated by R. Shamasastry

24. "Dharma Shastra: The Law Codes of Ancient India" by Patrick Olivelle

25. "Vrikshayurveda: The Science of Plant Life" translated by Nalini Sadhale

Additional Sources:

1. Bhagavad Gita: A spiritual text that synthesizes various streams of Indian philosophy, focusing on duty, ethics, and the path to liberation.
2. Puranas: Mythological texts that also contain historical, geographical, and cultural knowledge.

These references provide a comprehensive view of the Indian Knowledge System, covering a wide range of disciplines that have significantly influenced both Indian and global civilizations.